A-BW

ID397588

"The special bond we share with our family dog(s) is nurtured in this excellent 'how-to' book. Darlene writes with great compassion for the well-being of both ends of the human–animal bond."

—Alice Villalobos, D.V.M., A.A.H.A., hospital director of Veterinary Centers of America Coast Animal Hospital and Cancer Center; Editor-in-Chief, American Association of Human–Animal Bond Veterinarians Newsletter

"Both experienced and novice dog owners alike will love this resource and benefit from the valuable, comprehensive information."

—Merry Christine Crimi, D.V.M., hospital director, Gladstone Veterinary Clinics

"With excellent specialist resources, Darlene Arden has provided the one resource every owner should have on the bookshelf and consult often."

—Cheryl S. Smith, author of *Quick Clicks: 40 Fast and Fun Behaviors to Train with a Clicker*

"This is a vital reference work for any dog owner who wants to be able to understand what is really wrong with their dog, and to understand the medical jargon. Even better, it contains tips that may help you keep your dog out of the veterinarian's office in the first place."

—Stanley Coren, author of *How to Speak Dog* and *The Pawprints of History*

"With her latest book, Darlene Arden's partnership with the prestigious Angell Memorial Animal Hospital provides dog lovers with a fail-safe recipe for preventive care and wellness. Caring, creative, complete—this book rates a 'Best in Show'!"

—Amy D. Shojai, author of *Pet Care in the New Century* and *The First-Aid Companion for Dogs and Cats*

"Darlene Arden has filled a huge void with this book. Clear, concise, and easy to read, the balance of health, behavior, and general-care matters means that there is something for all."

—Martyn Blackmore, Director of Training and Behavior, Thousandoaks Dog Behaviour Services, United Kingdom

"The range of topics covered, well-identified 'tips' sections, and clear descriptions of technical veterinary terms make this wellness book a wonderful resource for any dedicated dog owner, though I suspect it will be in the libraries of most veterinarians as well."

—Dr. Alan M. Beck, Dorothy N. McAllister Professor of Animal Ecology and director of the Center for the Human–Animal Bond, School of Veterinary Medicine, Purdue University

"Author Darlene Arden has a special gift for translating veterinary terms and concepts into plain English. In this appealing work, she offers the reader what feels like a personal consultation with the expert veterinarians of Boston's legendary Angell Memorial Animal Hospital. Darlene Arden and 'Angell's angels' are a winning combination. Highly recommended!"

—Susan Conant, author of *The Dogfather* and *The Wicked Flea*

The Angell Memorial Animal Hospital

BOOK *of* WELLNESS

and PREVENTIVE

CARE *for* DOGS

The Angell Memorial Animal Hospital

BOOK of WELLNESS
and PREVENTIVE
CARE for DOGS

DARLENE ARDEN

Edited by Paul C. Gambardella, V.M.D., M.S., Diplomate, A.C.V.S.,

Chief of Staff, 1989–2001; Douglas Brum, D.V.M., Director of the Wellness and

Preventive Care Program; and the Veterinarians of Angell Memorial Animal Hospital

Foreword by Gus W. Thornton, D.V.M., President, MSPCA

Contemporary Books

Chicago   New York   San Francisco   Lisbon   London   Madrid   Mexico City
Milan   New Delhi   San Juan   Seoul   Singapore   Sydney   Toronto

The McGraw·Hill Companies

Library of Congress Cataloging-in-Publication Data

Arden, Darlene.
    The Angell Memorial Animal Hospital book of wellness and preventive care for
dogs / Darlene Arden ; foreword by Gus W. Thornton.
       p.   cm.
    ISBN 0-07-138489-8
    1. Dogs.   2. Dogs—Health.   3. Dogs—Diseases.   I. Title: Book of
wellness and preventive care for dogs.   II. Angell Memorial Animal Hospital
(Jamaica Plain, Boston, Mass.)   III. Title.

SF427 .A724   2002
636.7'0893—dc21   2002073716

1 2 3 4 5 6 7 8 9 0 AGM/AGM 1 0 9 8 7 6 5 4 3 2

ISBN 0-07-138489-8

Interior design by Susan H. Hartman
Interior illustrations copyright © Mary Jung, except p. 33 and p. 200 copyright © The
Massachusetts Society for the Prevention of Cruelty to Animals

McGraw-Hill books are available at special quantity discounts to use as premiums and
sales promotions, or for use in corporate training programs. For more information, please
write to the Director of Special Sales, Professional Publishing, McGraw-Hill, Two Penn
Plaza, New York, NY 10121-2298. Or contact your local bookstore.

This book is printed on acid-free paper.

For my mother,
who first taught me about unconditional love . . .
with my unconditional love.

Contents

Foreword

The *Angell Memorial Animal Hospital Book of Wellness and Preventive Care for Dogs* is a must-read for both new and veteran pet owners. Having been on staff at Angell for forty-five years and chief of staff for more than twenty years, I know the critical importance of wellness and preventive care. Ensuring that your dog is well protected against infectious diseases, well groomed, spayed or neutered, and well mannered is important to your pet's health and ability to be a great companion. A healthy and well-nourished pet has a greater chance of successful treatment when disease or injury do occur.

Experienced author Darlene Arden has presented wellness and preventive care in this book in an interesting, easy-to-read, and informative way. Because of her access to the multidisciplined staff at Angell, the information is also current and accurate.

Angell Memorial Animal Hospital is proud to have its name associated with this exciting addition to the dog owner's library.

Gus W. Thornton, D.V.M.
President, MSPCA

Acknowledgments

I am exceedingly grateful to those who have supported me as I wrote this book—first and foremost, Drs. Paul Gambardella and Douglas Brum, the staff of Angell Memorial Animal Hospital, the executives at the Massachusetts Society for the Prevention of Cruelty to Animals (MSPCA), and the American Humane Education Society. I'd like to acknowledge Barbara Castleman, Carey Yaruss, Lucinda DePatto, and especially the MSPCA's vice president of the Division of Health and Hospitals, Peter Theran, V.M.D., Diplomate, A.C.V.I.M. I am in awe of all that you do to help the animals.

A special thank-you to my remarkable friends Karen Overall, M.A., V.M.D., Ph.D.; and Raymond Russo, D.V.M., M.S., A.C.V.N. And thanks to Lea-Ann Germinder, Karen Pryor, and Alice Villalobos, D.V.M. Thanks also to Link Welborn, D.V.M., Diplomate, A.B.V.P., and Derek Woodbury of the American Animal Hospital Association.

My thanks to Debbi Baker, Lynne Rutenberg, and to my friends and colleagues, Amy D. Shojai and Cheryl S. Smith.

I want to thank my delightful and talented editor, Michele Pezzuti; my production editor, Ellen Vinz; and my agent, Meredith Bernstein, who makes it possible for me to concentrate on what I do best.

And thanks to all of the dogs who have graced my life and enriched it by their presence; they are not forgotten.

About Angell Memorial Animal Hospital

Founded in 1868, the Massachusetts Society for the Prevention of Cruelty to Animals (MSPCA) is one of the nation's oldest and most effective humane societies in the United States. Through its programs in veterinary medicine, sheltering, law enforcement, and advocacy, the MSPCA provides hands-on direct services to nearly 250,000 animals per year, more than any other humane organization.

Angell Memorial Animal Hospital was established in 1915 as a new division of the MSPCA and its educational affiliate, the American Humane Education Society (AHES). From its beginning, Angell's mission has been to provide the best possible medical and surgical care to animals and to advance the practice of veterinary medicine to an even higher standard.

During the past eighty-seven years, Angell has earned a reputation as an international center for excellence in clinical veterinary medicine. The hospital has many clinical specialties, including surgery, radiology, cardiology, dentistry, internal medicine, ophthalmology, avian and exotic medicine, dermatology, oncology, neurology, nutrition, and a full-service clinical pathology laboratory. The staff includes thirty-five staff veterinarians, thirteen interns, and fifteen residents, with total staff numbering about 325. Nearly fifty thousand cases come through the hospital each year.

The Intensive Care Unit, Intermediate Care Unit, Cancer Care Center, Emergency Services, and Wellness programs are examples of how Angell Memorial Animal Hospital continually strives to provide cutting-edge medical care for its patients. Through its internship and residency programs, Angell fulfills an important role as a teaching hospital in veterinary medicine, preparing the next generation of clinical scholars to be leaders in the profession.

Introduction

The day you bring your new dog home is full of excitement and promise. You know that you're ready for the responsibility a new pet will entail and you're willing to do the training necessary to make that new canine companion, from puppy to adult, a well-socialized, well-mannered family member. Ideally, you've chosen your pet carefully to ensure that you're well equipped to meet his particular needs. No doubt you bring that newcomer home expecting a long and happy life together.

A new approach in veterinary medicine seeks to ensure that long and happy life: *wellness*. Maintaining a healthy lifestyle and *preventing* problems before they start is a much wiser course of action than waiting until there's a problem to seek veterinary care.

The human medical profession has long realized that preventive health care programs can help people live longer, healthier lives, and the veterinary medical community is now recognizing the same benefits for pets. Angell Memorial Animal Hospital was one of the first veterinary institutions to initiate a wellness program for pets.

One benefit of wellness programs is flexibility—care is customized for each individual dog and owner's lifestyle. For example, people living in cities have different considerations than people who live in suburbs or rural areas. The breed of dog is an important consideration in building the program, as individual breeds are predisposed to particular health problems.

Angell's Wellness and Preventive Care program is divided into three life stages:

- The *puppy* stage includes the first year of the dog's life.
- The *adult* stage begins at one year and continues until the dog becomes a senior.
- *Senior* status differs for dogs according to size: the smaller the dog, the longer its lifespan. Small dogs (less than twenty pounds) are considered seniors at twelve years; medium dogs (twenty-one to fifty pounds) at eleven years; large dogs (fifty-one to ninety pounds) at eight years; and Giant breeds (more than ninety pounds) are seniors at seven years. Note that these classifications are based on the dog's normal, healthy weight, not the weight of an obese dog.

With this book, the world-renowned veterinarians of Angell Memorial Animal Hospital will help you and your veterinarian plan a wellness program for your pets. The tools are here for your pets to live a longer and healthier life.

PART I

Puppyhood

In the Beginning

Your puppy's first six months will have profound
effects on his health and behavior throughout his life.
Owning a dog is a big responsibility, so it's a good
idea to educate yourself before you get your dog.
Taking the time to research your dog's health needs
will be critically important in providing a
great start for your new life together.
—*Douglas Brum, D.V.M.*

Bringing a new canine companion into your life is a wonderful
adventure, and it's important to start off on the right foot. Now
that you've done your homework and chosen the right dog for
your lifestyle, it's time to choose your dog's veterinarian. Your initial visit
to your veterinarian's office is the beginning of a relationship that could
last throughout your dog's life. It sets the stage for a lifetime of good care.
(Note that although we will generally refer to puppies in this section of
the book, much of the information given here is applicable to newly
acquired adult dogs as well. We'll discuss issues related specifically to adult
dogs in Part II.)

Ideally you should schedule this initial appointment to occur two to three days after bringing your dog home. It's best not to do it within the first twenty-four hours, as there will be enough confusion in the dog's life while he's adjusting to his new surroundings.

Tricks of the Trade

Some states have puppy "lemon laws" stating that you can get your money back if something is discovered to be wrong with the pet within forty-eight to seventy-two hours of purchase, and guaranteeing some remuneration if the dog shows genetic defects at maturity.

Choosing Your Doctor

The first step, of course, is to choose a good veterinarian. Ask your friends with pets which doctors they recommend, and encourage them to be as specific as possible about what they like and don't like in various doctors. Another option is to contact your local humane society or animal shelter for names of reputable veterinarians.

You should choose a veterinarian with whom you have a good rapport. Open, two-way communication fosters a sense of continuity and trust. It's also vital in monitoring your dog's health—as your veterinarian becomes familiar with your dog over time, she will be all the better equipped to address the dog's particular needs.

There are things you can do to enhance the relationship you and your dog have with your veterinarian. For example, if your doctor is open to it, take your pet on occasional social visits to the office to help him bond with the staff. They will likely have treats on hand to give him, or you can bring a snack you know he likes and hand it to staff members for feeding. This type of visit can help your dog associate the veterinary hospital with happiness, which should make him feel that he's "among friends" during his medical visits. This will also make it easier for your veterinarian to care for your canine companion.

Another important way to encourage good communication with your veterinarian is to get in tune with your dog. You need to be able to tell when he's not feeling well and adequately explain the problem; after all, he cannot speak for himself. Your responsibility is to be your puppy's advocate.

TIPS FOR CHOOSING A GOOD VETERINARIAN

- Ask your breeder or a friend or neighbor who they would recommend.
- Make an appointment to meet the veterinarian and tour the hospital.
- Is the hospital clean? Does it smell clean (beyond the usual pet odors)?
- Can you easily communicate with the veterinarian? You will have to be your dog's advocate since he can't speak for himself.
- Does the veterinarian enjoy working with your particular breed or size of dog?
- If your dog is small, does the veterinarian moderate his or her touch for a smaller animal and does he or she move more slowly when working with a smaller dog?
- Will the veterinarian's office hours fit into your schedule?
- Does the veterinarian have emergency hours or will he or she refer you to an emergency practice so precious time isn't lost?
- If your pet must stay overnight, is there someone on duty in case of a problem?
- Does the veterinarian accept pet health insurance?
- What sorts of payment options are available?

The First Visit

When you go to your first veterinary appointment with your new dog, bring along any paperwork that you've received from the previous owner

THE ANGELL MODEL

One goal of this book is to show you how Angell Memorial Animal Hospital's Wellness and Preventive Care program works so that you and your veterinarian may adapt principles of Angell's program for your dog and your lifestyle.

Things work just a little bit differently at Angell because of the teaching hospital's structure. Although there is a full-time wellness veterinarian on staff whose only job is to work in the Wellness Clinic, veterinary interns rotate through the Wellness Clinic, so clients do not generally see the same veterinarian at each visit. Because of the number of veterinarians staffing the clinic, Angell needed to develop a system that would

- give clients the same education, guidance, and information at each visit;
- bring continuity to wellness care; and
- ensure the most up-to-date and comprehensive information is given to dog owners with healthy animals.

In order to accomplish this goal, they created the position of a full-time *preventive medicine technician* (PMT), also known as the *wellness technician*, who works with the clients and the veterinarians at each wellness visit. The PMT offers clients a sense of continuity and a familiar face.

The PMT is also the person who provides the routine client education at Angell, armed with a client checklist to ensure that the client receives the appropriate information and educational materials at each visit. There is a different checklist for each stage of the dog's life—puppy, adult, and senior—for each wellness visit, each one covering a different aspect of well animal care and responsible pet ownership. By following the checklist, Angell staff can be assured that clients are receiving information at the appropriate time in their dogs' health care plans.

(breeder, shelter, or rescue group, for example), including vaccination history. It's a good idea to make a copy of this paperwork for your own records before giving it to the veterinarian.

Your dog will be placed on the floor or on the examination table for his exam. Examination tables are made of cold steel and can be unpleasant for a dog—in fact, small dogs will always find it uncomfortable because they lose body heat more rapidly than larger dogs. The veterinarian may place a disposable cardboard crate mat on the examination table in order to minimize any discomfort. Your dog's earliest experiences at the veterinary hospital will be remembered, so you want them to be good ones. Be calm and cheerful during your dog's veterinary visits, and he will be, too.

The doctor or assistant will weigh the dog and take his temperature using either a rectal thermometer or an *ototympanic* (ear) thermometer. The ototympanic thermometer is far less stressful for the dog, but it is more expensive for the veterinarian and is less accurate than the rectal thermometer. Your veterinarian can show you how to take your dog's temperature at home. (See Chapter 11 for a brief description of this procedure.) When your dog is ill, knowing his temperature and relating that information to the veterinarian when you phone can be helpful. The average normal temperature for an adult dog is between 99.5 and 102.5 degrees Fahrenheit.

The physical examination should be gentle, and your veterinarian should show patience as she checks for inherited (*congenital*) abnormalities by gently examining the dog with her hands (*palpation*) and a stethoscope, and looking at his eyes, ears, mouth, skin, and coat. Common initial physical examination findings include umbilical hernias, undescended testicles (*cryptorchidism*), heart murmurs, ear and skin infections, and fleas.

The doctor should observe the newcomer to ensure that he moves normally, and determine whether he is alert and curious or withdrawn and shy. Under the best of circumstances your doctor will want to see whether the dog will come to him, perhaps enticed by a treat. This allows the dog to meet the veterinarian with a positive and curious attitude about the new human. The veterinarian, in turn, will go slowly and gain the puppy's trust. Since this first visit will set the tone for all future visits, it's important that it be a positive experience.

Keeping a Wellness Health Record

The key to an effective wellness program is that the pet owner and veterinarian work together to ensure the pet's health. Education is a vital aspect of that partnership, including handouts and instruction from the veterinarian or a veterinary technician. The more you know, the better you will be able to care for your pet.

At Angell, a wellness health record is begun for new dogs at the first visit. Each client is given a folder in which to store handouts and medical records. If your veterinarian doesn't give you a similar folder, you can certainly buy a folder and store all of your canine companion's records in it. This will be quite handy during your dog's lifetime because you'll always know where you can find everything you need pertaining to your dog's health.

Common Tests

The veterinary hospital may request that you bring a small stool sample to their facility so they may check for internal parasites. Puppies are especially at risk for intestinal worms, which they may have gotten from their mother, so routine fecal exams are important. It's not an unreasonable practice for puppies to be wormed routinely, *initially* every two to three weeks when they're quite young, even if their fecal tests are negative. Aside from the health implications of worms to your dog, some worms (mainly roundworms and hookworms) can cause *zoonotic diseases* (diseases that may be transmitted to people, especially young children). This is very uncommon, but it's better to be safe than sorry. A routine worming procedure should probably be in place in every wellness and preventive care program. Most breeders already have an appropriate worming program.

WELLNESS HEALTH RECORD CHECKLIST

Following are listed all the items Angell clients receive for their wellness health record. The preventive medicine technician reviews them with the client. Your veterinarian may have something similar or may have brochures in the waiting room.

First Visit

- "Welcome to Angell" brochure describing hospital services
- Health record
- Information on the individual vaccines that are recommended
- List of possible adverse vaccine reactions
- Information on puppy obedience and application for obedience classes
- Puppy feeding guide and phone number for nutritional advice
- Puppy health guide and food sample

Second Visit

- Handout describing heartworm disease
- Additional detailed information on obedience and training
- Dental care information and dental supplies and samples
- PennHip information (for dogs at risk of hip dysplasia)

Third Visit

- MSPCA information about spaying and neutering
- Grooming handout and information about how grooming enhances dogs' health, behavior, and training
- Information on how to control external parasites (parasites that live on an animal's hair or skin, as opposed to internal parasites such as heartworm)
- Information regarding the incidence and dangers of rabies and the importance of vaccination
- Animal ID program information, including tattoo and microchip information

Giardia

Puppies also should be tested for *giardia*, a zoonotic disease caused by a parasite. The veterinarian needs to look specifically for giardia because it won't always show up in the routine fecal examination. To detect giardia, your veterinarian will have to do either a zinc sulfate test or an *ELISA* (enzyme-linked amino-absorbent assay) test. In some professional veterinary publications it's said that a number of puppies will have giardia, but most show no signs of illness. The most common symptom is diarrhea.

Depending on where you live, your veterinarian may want to include a vaccination for giardia, though it is not currently recommended by or available at Angell. Since giardia reside in a wide variety of water sources, outdoor dogs are at higher risk, as are hunting dogs. Most dogs show no symptoms (that is, they are *asymptomatic*) but some puppies, older pets, or those with a compromised immune system might be at higher risk for more serious disease effects. (We will discuss giardia further in Chapter 2.)

Heartworm

Heartworm testing will not be done before the puppy is at least six months old. It takes about six months for a puppy to test positive for heartworm once he's infected. At Angell, puppies younger than six months are started on preventive medications, and those older than six months get the heartworm blood test. (We'll talk more about heartworm in Chapter 2.)

Vaccination

Your puppy will receive several vaccines that are commonly called *core vaccines*. These are given to every puppy and form the core of his protection from contagious diseases. They include distemper, parvovirus, hepatitis, rabies, and parainfluenza, and may also include leptospirosis (lepto).

Booster shots are generally given every three to four weeks until the puppy is four to five months old. Some consider leptospirosis to be a core vaccine, but most do not, so it is more commonly being considered a non-core vaccine.

Some recommend waiting for thirty minutes after your puppy's or dog's vaccination has been administered before going home, just in case there's an adverse reaction. Although severe reactions are rare, it is probably safest to wait. Typical vaccination reactions include mild lethargy and soreness at the vaccination site. But there can be more acute reactions. Occasionally, a fairly rapid facial swelling or hives on the skin may be noted. If this occurs, the dog will need to be treated.

Rarely an anaphylactic reaction may occur. This is the most severe type of reaction, and usually occurs rapidly (within thirty minutes). Symptoms include shortness of breath or trouble breathing, weakness, extreme lethargy, and even collapse. A dog may go into shock or even die if treatment is not provided rapidly. Fortunately, dogs typically respond well to treatment. It would be wise to reevaluate your dog's vaccination protocol in light of any serious vaccine reactions. Pretreating dogs with medications to decrease the potential of reactions prior to vaccinations or omitting certain vaccinations should be considered.

Types of Vaccines

There are different types of vaccines. The *live vaccine*, which is made from the active virus, is rarely used today. Following are the three most common vaccines currently in use:

Modified live. The virus is altered so it is no longer virulent to the dog but will help the dog's body create an immunity to the virus.

Killed. The virus itself has been deactivated, so it is safer than the modified live because the virus cannot reproduce itself. The problem, however, is that the killed vaccine requires an *adjuvant* (a substance enhancing the immune response to an antigen) to make it more effective.

Subunit. This vaccine is not infectious and contains only the parts of the microorganism that are necessary to yield the desired protective immune response. This vaccine is generally considered both safe and effective.

Recombinant vaccines are new and are created by using specific DNA of the organism. Since the recombinant vaccine doesn't require an adjuvant to activate it, it can be a very good choice. This appears to be the wave of the future.

Also new are the *high-titer modified live vaccines*, which are given to puppies in an attempt to provide quicker and more effective protection specifically from parvovirus infections. When a puppy is born he receives protective antibodies from his mother that slowly decrease over time. At first these antibodies protect against disease, but as their concentration decreases the puppy becomes susceptible to infection. Unfortunately, the maternal antibodies acquired when nursing the mother's initial milk (called *colostrum*) also block the effectiveness of the vaccines, and thus there is usually a period of time when the vaccines are not effective, the maternal antibodies are no longer protective, and the puppy is at risk of contracting the disease. The goal of the high-titer vaccines is to achieve vaccine protection at an earlier age and to decrease the window of opportunity of disease transmission.

Distemper

Distemper, which affects the respiratory and nervous systems, is a viral disease that's highly contagious among dogs. It's transmitted from dog to dog by contact with fecal matter, urine, or eye or nasal discharges. Most dogs that contract distemper will die from it, and puppies are at even higher risk. In such a weakened condition, it's easy for a dog to contract a secondary ailment such as pneumonia. A dog who survives distemper will usually be left with residual neurological damage. The dog could lose sight, smell, or hearing, or could be partially paralyzed. Symptoms of distemper include vomiting, diarrhea, weight loss, coughing, and nasal discharge—so it could easily be mistaken for something else, thereby delaying diagnosis and treatment.

If a dog survives distemper he will be immune for the rest of his life. All dogs should be vaccinated for distemper with periodic booster shots. Consult your veterinarian about how often your own dog should be vaccinated for this disease. And at the first sign of any illness, do take him to the veterinarian. The disease is so prevalent that most dogs come into contact with it. Whatever ails your dog, a quick trip to your veterinarian can assure you of prompt diagnosis and treatment.

Hepatitis

Hepatitis (*adenovirus*), another infectious viral disease, used to be a much more common disease before a vaccine was developed, but vaccination has virtually eliminated it. The adenovirus used to cause inflammation of the liver, which would eventually lead to liver failure. Occasionally it would cause corneal edema (a bluish tinge to the cornea) and lead to blindness.

Parainfluenza

Parainfluenza is a highly contagious respiratory disease that may spread quickly among dogs. It is caused by a virus and is one of the agents responsible for causing "kennel cough." The virus produces inflammation of the windpipe (trachea). Most dogs will have a dry hacking cough that usually improves without treatment (or sometimes with only a cough suppressant). If the coughing does not improve, a secondary bacterial pneumonia can ensue, which would be much more serious.

Bordatella

Bordatella, one of the causes of kennel cough, is a separate vaccination. The signs of this disease are similar to those of parainfluenza. Dogs that are frequently boarded are usually required (by the kennel or boarding place) to have a bordatella vaccination. Angell does not routinely administer a bordatella vaccine, but will give it to dogs at risk. The vaccine comes in two forms: *injectable* and *intranasal*. The more popular and effective intranasal vaccine, which gives more rapid protection, is sprayed into the dog's nose, which means it is more difficult to administer if the dog objects to the procedure. He might squirm, preventing himself from receiving the entire dose of vaccine, or he could sneeze it out.

Parvovirus

Your puppy will be vaccinated for parvovirus, which is a very serious contagious disease generally seen in puppies rather than adult dogs. It causes severe vomiting and diarrhea and suppresses the immune system. Severe cases of parvovirus may be fatal, even if treated. After the initial vaccination series, a blood test (parvo titer) can determine whether the dog has adequate protection. Parvovirus seems particularly to be a problem among Rottweilers, Doberman Pinschers, and Pit Bulls, so they might receive an extra parvo vaccination at five months of age. At the very least these dogs should have their blood checked to ensure adequate protection from the disease.

Rabies

Rabies is a serious public health concern. Mammals (such as raccoons, skunks, bats, foxes, dogs, and cats) can carry it and it can be transferred to humans. The virus is spread through wounds via the saliva of a rabid animal. Laws governing rabies vaccination vary from state to state. In Massachusetts, puppies receive their first rabies vaccination as early as three months of age, but usually between four and six months of age, with booster shots nine to twelve months later, and then every three years. Some states require an annual booster.

Symptoms of rabies include profound changes in behavior typical of the animal's species and individual personality—for example, foxes get friendly, or a gregarious dog may begin acting frightened—so it's important to know what behavior is normal for each species. Watch for overly vicious or timid behavior, lack of coordination, and difficulty swallowing. Once the symptoms appear, rabies is fatal.

A person who is known to have been exposed to rabies can be treated with a vaccination, but a person who begins to show symptoms of rabies cannot be treated. An animal that has been vaccinated against rabies may also be treated with a rabies vaccination after exposure, but an unvaccinated animal cannot be treated. A vaccinated dog is well protected from this dreaded disease.

Leptospirosis

Leptospirosis is an infectious disease that may cause severe liver and kidney damage and may also affect people. The disease can be seen at any age; it's very serious and often fatal. It is caused by a spirochete bacterium found commonly in the rat population. Dogs may be exposed to the bacterium through stagnant water that has been contaminated with rodent secretions. Dogs that live in the country or go hiking or camping are at increased risk of contracting the disease. However, leptospirosis is more prevalent in cities, where there is a high rodent population.

Vaccination does offer some protection against the disease, but it is not straightforward. The disease may be caused by different strains (or serotypes) of the bacteria. The vaccine must incorporate each serotype to be fully protective and there is no cross-protection from one serotype to another. For example, if a dog is vaccinated for serotypes "A" and "B" but then is exposed to serotype "C," he may become ill. There are five main serotypes of leptospirosis, and the typical vaccine only has two of these. This allows for potential cases of leptospirosis even in vaccinated animals. Fortunately, newer leptospirosis vaccines have been developed that have four of the serotypes, thus offering broader protection.

An additional complication of the leptospirosis vaccine is that it may only be effective for six months at a time and thus requires a booster every six months for year-long protection. Considering the vaccine's duration of protection and the multiple strains of the organism, it should not be surprising to learn that the disease is still seen in veterinary hospitals around the country.

The discussion to vaccinate, not vaccinate, or how often to vaccinate is a complex one. Factors such as lifestyle, breed, age, environment, and travel potential should all be taken into account when considering this vaccine. It should be discussed with your veterinarian. Many veterinarians do not have a set policy for leptospirosis vaccinations and will vaccinate based on the individual dog's risk factors.

Lyme Disease

While there is a vaccine for Lyme disease, it should be given only if a good reason exists to do so. It is better to have a preventive tick-control program (which we'll discuss further in Chapter 2) in place, but if you live in an area with a sizable tick population you and your veterinarian might consider administering the Lyme vaccine to your dog. It can be given to puppies twelve weeks of age or older in two doses that are given two to three weeks apart. An annual booster is recommended for those receiving the vaccine.

Coronavirus

The coronavirus vaccine is given by some veterinarians, though Angell does not recommend it for routine use. Coronavirus may cause diarrhea, or it may be *subclinical* (not detectable by clinical tests) or self-limiting, meaning that the dog can rid himself of the virus on his own without becoming ill. Most dogs become only mildly ill from the virus and recover on their own. Coronavirus may be of greater concern in breeding kennels or shelters.

Tricks of the Trade

Nothing about a wellness and preventive care program is written in stone—it must be customized for each dog, even more so for adult dogs than for puppies. But even the puppy's program will have to weigh risk factors that will differ for each puppy, depending on his breed and size and his owner's residence and lifestyle.

Nutrition

The first visit is a good time to discuss nutrition with your veterinarian so that you can make an informed decision about your dog's diet. Your veterinarian will give you appropriate feeding guidelines. If your puppy came from a responsible breeder, he's probably already eating a complete and balanced diet from a reputable company. Angell clients receive the phone number of a full-time staff veterinary nutritionist they may call for nutritional advice. We'll discuss nutrition in detail in Chapter 5.

Tricks of the Trade

A puppy's ration for a full day should be divided into multiple meals depending on his age. From weaning to three months of age, he should be offered four meals per day; from three to six months he should be offered three meals per day; from six months to one year, he may be fed two meals per day; and adult dogs may eat one or two meals per day. Smaller adult dogs seem to do quite well when their food is divided into two meals because their stomachs are smaller and can't handle a large portion of food efficiently at one time. Fresh water should be available to your dog at all times.

Grooming

Good grooming is an essential part of preventing external parasites, and keeping your dog clean will keep him healthier in general. Daily brushing and combing will not only prevent mats and tangles but will remove dead hair and dirt and stimulate blood supply to the skin, resulting in a healthier, shinier coat. We'll discuss grooming in greater detail in Chapter 3.

Your veterinarian will teach you how to feel your puppy for lumps and bumps, which you can easily do during your regular grooming session. Let your puppy become accustomed to your hands going over his body; it will make it easier for your veterinarian to examine him, which will make for a far more pleasant experience all around.

Dental Care

Your veterinarian will talk to you about the importance of dental care and will probably give you a sample of a special toothpaste made just for dogs. It doesn't foam, but it is flavored, which will make it more appealing to your little companion and thereby make the cleaning process more tolerable. (Never use toothpaste for humans on your dog!) Your veterinarian will teach you how to clean your dog's teeth, a process that will be discussed in detail in Chapter 3.

Spaying and Neutering

Spaying and neutering are important issues that your veterinarian will discuss with you at the first or second visit, likely setting up an appointment for the relatively simple procedure that should be done before sexual

HIP DYSPLASIA

At this time, Angell clients are given information about the *PennHip program*, which allows for earlier identification of dogs with potential for hip dysplasia (see Chapter 7, page 124). This is a debilitating disease. No dog who manifests it should ever be bred. And if your dog has it, it's better to take preventive measures, which include keeping the dog thin and well muscled, and to know which symptoms to look for.

maturity. At Angell, this discussion usually takes place during the second visit.

Unless you are a responsible dog breeder who is doing all of the applicable genetic testing and showing your dogs—in other words, unless you have secured objective and educated opinions that your dogs meet the standard for their breed—you should not think about creating more puppies and exacerbating the pet overpopulation problem. Not only are there too many dogs without homes, but there is no need to add to the purebred

REASONS TO SPAY OR NEUTER YOUR DOG

Female Dogs

- Spaying greatly reduces the risks of ovarian and mammary cancers. Spaying before her first heat cycle will reduce these risks even further.
- Spaying prevents *Pyometra*, an infection of the uterus that is a very serious health risk in older, unspayed female dogs.
- Spaying prevents her heat cycles, which will allow her to have a safer, happier life. This also prevents damage to your furniture and carpeting from heat cycle discharge.
- Spaying prevents unwanted litters from being born! There are so many puppies in shelters already; finding good, loving homes for more puppies is a burden on your time and finances, and the lives of innocent dogs.

Male Dogs

- Neutering helps prevent tumors and hernias of the testicles.
- Neutering helps prevent a variety of prostatic diseases such as infections, abscesses, and cysts, which occur under the influence of testosterone.
- Neutering will curb his aggressive/hyperactive nature at puberty. This will alleviate tendencies toward biting, urine marking, and aggressive and dominant behavior around other dogs and people.
- Neutering will *not* change your dog's favorable behaviors, such as playfulness, friendliness, and socialization with other dogs and people.

From the Animal Wellness Program at Angell Memorial Animal Hospital

population unless it is to better the breed. There are far too many genetic problems that may be inherited, problems that can be both heartbreaking and costly. Sometimes the mother dies while whelping a litter, or requires a cesarean section. Most pet owners don't consider the potential risks, complications, and expense of raising a litter. Reputable and responsible breeders lose money on every litter they breed.

Another important reason for spaying or neutering before sexual maturity concerns the health of your dog. Neutering cuts the risk of testicular cancer to zero and significantly decreases the incidence of prostate disease later in life. Spaying a female dog before the first or second heat also lowers the incidence of uterine infection, uterine and ovarian cancer, and mammary cancer. Spaying will also eliminate the arrival on your

THE IMPORTANCE OF BEING OBEDIENT

GOOD BEHAVIOR CAN MEAN A LIFETIME OF LOVE

Why are countless numbers of dogs abandoned, surrendered to shelters, or put to death every day?

Experience at MSPCA shelters indicates that the most common reason long-term owner-pet relationships fail is lack of commitment. Something happens after we take that adorable little puppy into our homes—that puppy grows into a dog that, without training, acts like a dog. Many people find it difficult to maintain a committed relationship with a seventy–five–pound animal that has no social skills. Things that were cute when the dog was small, such as jumping up, barking for attention, running away, pulling on the leash, and having accidents on the brand-new rug are no longer so endearing when the dog is an adult.

These are examples of normal canine behaviors that do not fit well into a human family. Sadly, when these behaviors are not controlled, they can result in the surrender of the dog to a shelter. A shelter is not the ideal environment in which to train and socialize a dog, but a family is.

Angell Memorial veterinarians and MSPCA staff have come to believe that if common behavior problems can be prevented or controlled, many more happy doorstep of every male dog in the neighborhood whenever your female dog is in heat. Angell will spay or neuter as early as ten weeks of age.

You need not fear that your pet will grow fat and lazy after being neutered, though it's always important to maintain a proper diet and exercise regimen throughout your pet's life to maximize his health and longevity.

At the time you bring your puppy to be spayed or neutered, the dog will likely receive a parvo vaccine if needed (based on the parvo titer or risks of the specific breed). The dog may possibly be tattooed or microchipped (for verifiable permanent identification in case he is ever lost or stolen), as these procedures can be done while the dog is under

---

dogs and owners will remain together, and many fewer pets will be given up. The MSPCA conducts classes on our premises that deal with everyday situations. All of our classes teach, in the easiest way for both you and your dog, the essential obedience commands of *sit, stay, down, heel,* and *come.*

If you teach a puppy before he has learned bad behaviors, such as jumping, pulling on the leash, and running away, it is much easier. You do not have to break the bad habits first. Our puppy workshops, for dogs between eight and nineteen weeks of age, help address puppy-related problems such as housebreaking, chewing, biting, and jumping. The classes help socialize the puppies with other dogs and people. Our companion classes for dogs over nineteen weeks handle such common adult problems as jumping up, running away, and excitement around other dogs. This class ends with the Canine Good Citizen test.

Our teachers will also teach you how to take proper preventive care of your dog. Included are nutrition, grooming, and home health exams.

Above all, our classes will give you a good dose of understanding why your four-legged friend does what he does. Experience has shown that understanding leads to appreciation and commitment. Commitment is the most important element in ensuring that your relationship with your dog will be happy, loving, and long lasting.

From the Animal Wellness Program at Angell Memorial Animal Hospital

anesthesia for spaying or neutering. It's ideal to have a more permanent method of identifying your pet to accompany his collar and tags.

Obedience Training

Your dog will be a better companion if he is well trained, so enrolling him in obedience classes is a smart thing to do. Training your puppy properly, using the gentlest, most positive methods, will make him a joy to live with.

A puppy who is not trained may grow into an unmanageable dog, no matter how big or small he is—and an unmanageable dog usually ends up in a shelter or rescue because the owners simply cannot cope with him. Training is a responsibility you assume when you choose to bring a dog into your life.

A clicker training kit is available to Angell clients. This is an easy, humane, simple, and fun way to teach your dog to become a happy, responsive, well-mannered companion. The kit includes an informational handout about clicker training along with a complimentary clicker—a small device that gives the dog a consistent auditory cue when he responds correctly to your commands. Clients can also purchase a small, easy-to-follow booklet that teaches clients how to train their dog using a clicker.

The classes at Angell Memorial have been created not for performance obedience but for good behavior in everyday situations. Included, of course, are the essentials: *sit, stay, down, heel,* and *come.* Most puppy train-

PET HEALTH INSURANCE

You will want to discuss pet health insurance early on. It can make a big difference in whether you can afford an expensive procedure that your dog may need later in life. There are several pet health insurance companies offering different programs. Talk with your veterinarian about which ones she recommends and then make the choice that's right for you and your dog.

ing classes will help with such problems as housetraining, chewing, biting, and jumping.

A dog can begin training at any age, so if you have adopted an older dog, it's not too late. It may take a little longer than it would with a puppy, but it will be well worth the effort. In fact, training is a wonderful way for you and your dog to have fun together. Adult dog obedience classes address common adult problems like jumping up, chasing, and aggression. We'll discuss training and behavior problems further in Chapter 6.

Happily, you and your puppy or dog are well on your way to having a long, healthy life together.

What We've Learned

Adjuvant: A substance added to a vaccine to stimulate it

Asymptomatic: Showing no symptoms

Colostrum: Mother's initial milk

Congenital: Referring to inherited genetic traits

Core vaccines: Shots given to all puppies to protect them against common diseases

Cryptorchidism: Undescended testicles

ELISA test: Enzyme-linked amino-absorbent assay test

Ototympanic thermometer: Thermometer that is inserted in the ear

Palpation: Examining by touch, especially medically

Zoonotic: Referring to diseases that may be transmitted between animals and humans

2

Controlling and Preventing Parasites

Anyone who owns a dog is going to encounter
parasites sooner or later; they're simply a fact of
canine life. The bad news about parasites is that
they often are hidden from view, but can cause serious
disease in your pet. The good news is that new drugs
are available that are very effective at prevention
and treatment. Veterinarians will recommend these
drugs for your pet for good reasons — take advantage
of them to keep your pet parasite-free.

— *Peter Theran, V.M.D.,*
Diplomate, A.C.V.I.M.

Where there are dogs, there will always be opportunistic parasites seeking a host. They cause stress and aggravation for
both the dog and the owner. Some diseases of parasites are
zoonotic, and that's only one reason why it's best to prevent parasites before
they become a treatment problem.

Two basic types of parasites exist: *internal* and *external*. Internal parasites are those that live inside your dog, such as giardia, hookworm,

roundworm, tapeworm, heartworm, and coccidia. External parasites include fleas, mites, and ticks, which latch onto the dog, suck her blood, and may even transfer disease to the dog through the bloodstream. Internal parasites are referred to as an *infection*, while external parasites are referred to as an *infestation*.

Parasites and the diseases they carry could fill an entire book by themselves. We'll discuss some of the most common ones here.

Internal Parasites

Internal parasites can make your canine companion very sick, causing diarrhea, nausea, vomiting, and anemia. Most can be detected by examination of a stool sample, which is why you should bring one with you every time you take your puppy to the veterinarian.

Puppies are often born with intestinal parasites that have been passed along to them by their mother. Roundworms (*ascarids*) are the most common. It is recommended that all puppies be routinely dewormed for ascarids and hookworms, which are also quite common, both before and during the vaccination period. Adult dogs usually develop a resistance to most intestinal parasites, except whipworms (*Trichuris vulpis*), which can cause intestinal problems, leading to symptoms of colitis (inflammation of the colon).

Roundworms

Roundworm is usually found in young dogs, as many puppies contract the parasite from their mother in utero or while nursing. Dogs may also contract roundworm by ingesting infected rodents or dirt with infective worm eggs (usually through normal licking and grooming).

Roundworms can measure up to 7 inches (18 centimeters), and a female can lay up to a hundred thousand eggs per day. Roundworm infection is considered a zoonotic disease, meaning that roundworms can be transferred to people. (Small children are more commonly affected than adults.)

Once contracted, roundworms take up residence in the small intestine. Puppies may show no signs, or only mild signs, of infection; those with moderate to heavy infections look potbellied and malnourished, have a tender abdomen, and may have diarrhea, constipation, or vomiting. An infected dog's intestines could become impacted or perforated, a condition that can be fatal.

Diagnosis is made via clinical and fecal examination. Treatment includes very safe and effective antiparasitic drugs (*anthelmintics*). A repeat treatment is given ten to twenty days later. If a puppy is very ill from this infection, he might also require intravenous fluid and nutritional support.

Tricks of the Trade

Bring a small stool sample to every veterinary visit to ensure routine microscopic screening for parasites.

Coccidia

Coccidia is another parasite that infects the intestine. It is found in the ground and ingested when, for example, a dog licks herself after walking through an infected area or licks grass. The parasites reproduce inside the dog, rapidly multiplying in number.

Coccidia can spread quickly in a kennel or shelter, and is a problem mostly in puppies that are malnourished or ill from other diseases. It causes a watery, bloody diarrhea that may endanger a puppy's life.

Coccidia diagnosis is made via fecal examination; often it is found during a routine fecal exam of an otherwise healthy asymptomatic dog. Only the dog's own immune system can kill coccidia. If required, medication can be given that disrupts the reproduction of coccidia in the dog's intestine, thereby weakening the infection and giving the dog's immune system a better chance to eliminate it. Medication is given for five to fourteen days and may need to be repeated.

Giardia

Giardia is a protozoal parasite found in cyst form in bodies of water (for example, puddles, mountain streams, wastewater, floodwater, muddy creeks, wellwater, and swimming pools) and in animal feces. Once a dog ingests the cysts from a contaminated site, the cysts open inside the dog and take up residence and multiply in the intestines.

Dogs at increased risk of contracting giardia include those that

- Live outdoors
- Live on farms
- Hunt
- Are puppies
- Are in poor nutritional condition
- Have compromised immune systems
- Drink from rivers and streams

Diarrhea is the principal symptom of giardiasis, though most dogs that contract giardia are asymptomatic and will eventually cure themselves. Even an asymptomatic dog can still shed giardia cysts in feces, exposing other pets and humans to it.

Giardia is not normally found in routine fecal examinations. The cysts are quite small and usually require a special test for detection. Various drugs may be used to treat giardiasis, but they may need to be repeated. A vaccine is available to protect against giardia, but even vaccinated dogs may still shed giardia cysts. Discuss with your veterinarian whether the giardia vaccine is necessary for your dog.

As is so often the case with your pet's health, prevention is the best option. Try to keep your dog from drinking from questionable water sources. If you're hiking or walking with your dog, carry water and a collapsible dog dish with you to ensure a supply of fresh, clean water. Take water for yourself, too, since giardia is another zoonotic disease; people who hike or camp and drink from contaminated water can contract this parasite. At home, keep the toilet lid down to prevent transmission from people to dogs.

Tapeworm

Most tapeworm infections are obtained through flea infestations. Adult fleas carry tapeworm eggs, and the dog ingests the eggs when she inadvertently swallows an infected flea while biting at it or grooming. The eggs grow to maturity in the dog's small intestine, a process that takes less than a month. A dog might also contract tapeworms by eating an infected rodent.

The most obvious sign that your dog has tapeworms is the visible presence of the worms themselves—or rather, small segments of the worms that are passed through the stools. They look like grains of rice and are most commonly found around the dog's anus, in her bedding, or in her feces. Fortunately, tapeworms look worse than they really are. They rarely make dogs ill, but finding the small segments crawling around on one's dog often prompts a quick visit to the vet.

Generally speaking, preventing fleas is the key to preventing tapeworms. Treatment includes specific deworming medication that may not typically be given on a routine preventive treatment basis. The tapeworms often reappear quickly if the flea problem is not also addressed.

Hookworms

Hookworms are parasites that are so named for the hooklike structures in their mouths, which they use to attach to the intestines of their host. There are five different species of hookworms, and one female can produce up to twenty thousand eggs per day. A dog may become infected by the following means:

- Ingestion of soil or feces contaminated with hookworm larvae or eggs
- Penetration of the skin by hookworm larvae
- Transmission via an infected mother's bloodstream while in utero or milk while nursing

Hookworms suck blood from tiny vessels in the dog's intestinal wall, creating a danger of anemia. Infected dogs may lack energy or have pale gums or diarrhea. A small or moderate infection may produce mild inflammation of the intestines (*enteritis*). A heavy infection, especially in a small, young, or debilitated dog, can result in acute bloody diarrhea. The loss of blood can lead to anemia and possibly shock. Blood transfusions might be necessary in severe infections.

Hookworms are diagnosed by fecal examination. Heartworm preventive medication also effectively prevents hookworms. Infected dogs may be treated with medications that kill the adult hookworm; because it does not kill eggs or larvae, the medication must be repeated in three to four weeks to kill newly formed adult worms.

External Parasites

External parasites are abundant in the environment, so you should not be surprised if your dog plays host to a group of them. They can cause all manner of misery for your pets, from mild itching to serious skin disorders and infections. Therefore, you should take swift action to eliminate such pests.

Mites

Dogs can get mites as early as within seventy-two hours of birth, while nursing. The life cycle of a mite is between twenty and thirty-five days, and the mite spends all of that time on the dog.

Demodectic Mange (Demodicosis). Demodectic mange is caused by demodectic mites, which live within the hair follicles. It's normal for a small number of demodectic mites to live in the hair follicles of healthy dogs; *demodicosis* occurs when the dog's immune system can't control the number of mites. (Demodicosis is not contagious from dogs to people.) The localized type of mange appears as one or more small areas of bald spots (*alopecia*), sometimes with scaling; skin infection (*pyoderma*); and hyperpigmentation. It usually occurs on the head, neck, and front legs, although it can be seen on any area of the body.

The generalized form of demodicosis is seen mainly in dogs under eighteen months of age. The localized form is often a self-limiting disease and may not require therapy. A small number of localized cases may develop into generalized cases. The prognosis for generalized demodicosis, which is a more serious disease than localized demodicosis, depends on a variety of factors and will vary from case to case. In the past, insecticidal dips and caustic salves were the treatments of choice, but newer treatments have led to improved results. Discuss the options with your veterinarian and decide together which treatment is best for your dog.

Sarcoptic Mange (Canine Scabies). The microscopic adult mites that cause sarcoptic mange prefer skin to hair and are usually found on elbows, ears, and hocks. Scabies is highly contagious among dogs and is also zoonotic, with symptoms developing from ten days to eight weeks after initial contact is made. Intense itching (*pruritus*) is a major symptom, along with alopecia and eruptions that are covered with a thick yellow crust. Secondary lesions can bleed and develop bacterial infections. Discuss treatment options with your veterinarian.

Ear Mites. Ear mites may cause ear infections and are highly contagious from dog to dog. A dog with an ear mite infestation usually will scratch his ears and shake or tilt his head frequently. Diagnosis is made by swabbing the ears and examining the discharge microscopically; treatment consists of cleaning the ear thoroughly with a product recommended by your veterinarian. There are a variety of medications available.

Heartworm Disease

Heartworm is one of the first things your dog (if she is older than six months) will be tested for when you take her to the veterinarian. Once a blood test returns a negative result, your dog will be started on preventive

LOVE MAY NOT BE THE ONLY THING IN YOUR DOG'S HEART

PREVENTING AND TREATING HEARTWORM DISEASE

Heartworm disease is caused by a parasite that is becoming more common. While dogs and other members of the canine family (wolves, foxes, and coyotes, for example) are the primary hosts, other species can also be infected, including members of the cat family, muskrats, raccoons, bears, ferrets, and sea lions. The parasite is carried from one host to another by mosquitoes.

Heartworm exists only in geographic areas with a supply of primary hosts (dogs, for example) and mosquitoes. Although infection in humans has been reported, such cases are rare, and people can't pass the parasite on. Doctors do not consider human infection a serious condition.

A dog who is a host—or carrier—of heartworm may be completely free of symptoms or may show signs of severe illness. The earliest sign is usually a cough. Further signs include tiring with exercise, collapsing spells, and an enlarging abdomen due to heart failure. Severely infested dogs can die from heartworm.

Diagnosis

Heartworm disease is usually diagnosed by detecting first-stage larvae (*microfilariae*) in a sample of the dog's blood or by detecting antigens associated with heartworm in the dog's serum.

Treatment

Dogs who test positive for heartworm are first treated with intravenous injections of a drug containing arsenic to kill the adult worms. At a later date, additional medication will be required to eliminate the microfilariae.

Prevention

Medication to prevent heartworm is available. It is safe for dogs who test free of the disease. Young puppies can be given the medication without having a blood test, but dogs six months or older must be tested first.

Testing is very important, as 5 to 10 percent of infested dogs will have serious or even fatal reactions if they are given preventive medication.

Different types of heartworm medication can be given on a daily or monthly schedule. Ask your veterinarian which type is best for your dog. When used properly this medication is nearly 100 percent effective in preventing heartworm disease.

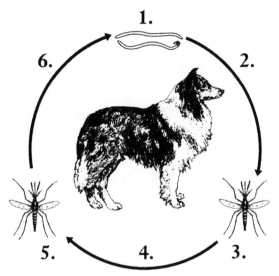

The Heartworm Life Cycle

1. The host dog has adult heartworms in the right side of the heart and the pulmonary arteries.
2. A fertile female heartworm releases first-stage, microscopic larvae (*microfilariae*) into the host dog's peripheral blood.
3. A mosquito bites the host dog, ingesting microfilariae.
4. In the mosquito, the microfilariae undergo two stages of development, becoming third-stage, or infective, larvae.
5. The mosquito bites another dog, injecting the infective larvae into the bite.
6. In the second dog, these larvae undergo two more developmental stages, called *moults*, and migrate to the right side of the heart and pulmonary arteries, where they mature to adults. Some microfilariae remain in the peripheral blood, making this dog a host.

The entire life cycle takes from seven to nine months.

From the Animal Wellness Program at Angell Memorial Animal Hospital

medication. It is vital that the dog take this medication as scheduled—heartworm is costly to cure and can be fatal. *But your dog should not begin using the medication until she has had the proper blood test first.*

Heartworms are found in virtually every state in the United States and throughout other areas of the world. Any dog can contract heartworm disease if left unprotected. Because heartworm disease is carried by mosquitoes, it's easy to assume that dogs spending most of their time indoors cannot contract it—but this simply isn't true, as mosquitoes can easily get into indoor areas.

When an infected mosquito bites the dog, it sucks blood from the dog and transfers the infectious agents into the dog's tissues. After migrating through the dog's system for about six months, the worms become adult heartworms living in the heart and producing offspring (*microfilariae*). The large worms grow within the dog's heart, which causes symptoms akin to those of a cardiac condition, including difficulty breathing, coughing, tiring easily, listlessness, weight loss, and a rough coat in a dog whose coat is normally smooth. The disease may not show symptoms in its early stages. The dog can develop heart failure and die if the disease is not treated.

The first heartworm preventive on the market was a daily pill that was given through the summer months only. Newer heartworm pills have been developed that prevent a broader spectrum of parasites and are given just once a month. Angell recommends giving year-round heartworm medication and/or strategic year-round worming. The year-round heartworm medication not only prevents heartworm and other parasites, it decreases the zoonotic potential of parasitic diseases (such as roundworm). That's why a dog should take once-a-month heartworm preventive medication throughout the winter even though she can't get heartworm in a cold climate.

A new injectible heartworm preventive called *moxidectin* is administered once every six months and may be used on dogs six months of age and older. This can prove particularly useful for owners who may not reliably remember to give the dog the monthly preventive pill. It should not be administered to sick, debilitated, or underweight dogs. Owners should be warned that a small palpable spot may appear under the skin at the injection site and assured that it's no cause for concern. And, of course, preexisting heartworm infections should be diagnosed and treated appropriately before starting the injectible preventive. Talk with your veterinarian to see whether moxidectin is appropriate for your dog. It may be more difficult to administer to dogs under five pounds, very large dogs, and dogs that are not fully grown. It's conceivable that under some circumstances, administering it to a growing dog might result in dilution of the active ingredient below effective levels by the end of the growth curve. In other words, if you're giving an injection based on the dog's weight that's supposed to last six months and the weight has doubled in three months, it may not be still working; you might not be giving an effective dose so it may not be as effective a choice for rapidly growing dogs.

Talk with your veterinarian about the risk of heartworm disease where you live and take appropriate measures.

Fleas

Probably the first example that comes to mind when you think of parasites is the flea. This little insect gives dogs and their owners a good deal of trouble and is responsible for the most common dermatological complaint: flea allergy dermatitis. A flea injects its saliva into a dog when it bites him, and that saliva prevents the dog's blood from coagulating. While some dogs aren't bothered by the saliva, others are allergic to it and scratch in an attempt to relieve discomfort.

The offensive little insects are tiny, brown, and capable of jumping great distances (as far as six inches). A pair of fleas can produce millions of offspring over their lives. The life cycle has four stages: adults lay *eggs* on the dog, which may stay to develop on the dog or drop off and develop where they land (for example, in your carpet). The eggs hatch, becoming *larvae*, which live in carpeting, cracks, and corners, surviving by ingesting dried blood, dander from animals, and other organic matter. Next, the larvae develop into *pupae*, which hatch into *adults*. The warmer and more humid the atmosphere, the faster this development will occur. Pupae can lie dormant for months and hatch when the climate is ideal. Your warm home can provide a perfect year-round environment for fleas, but these insects have survived for millions of years in a wide range of environments.

Some dogs infested with fleas, in addition to scratching, may chew frantically at themselves until they've created hairless spots that are red, raw, and weeping serum (*hot spots*). Scratching might also lead to widespread hair loss, redness, scaling, bacterial infection, or thickening and increased pigmentation of the skin. These problems are most commonly seen on the lower back, the base of the tail, the back of the thighs, part of the abdomen, flanks, and neck. In a severe case, the entire body can exhibit these symptoms. Additionally, fleas can carry tapeworms (see page 29).

Fleas feed on blood, so a small dog or puppy with a severe infestation can become anemic (this is more common in young puppies than in adults). She may also be lethargic and have pale lips and gums. It's possible for an infestation to be fatal.

Your dog may have a flea infestation even if you don't see the insects; fleas spend almost their entire life cycle off the pet. If your dog is scratching or has scabs, or if you find "flea dirt" (small black specks that resemble pepper) on her skin, you should suspect fleas. Flea dirt can be distinguished from regular dirt with a simple test: put it on a white paper towel or cotton ball and lightly moisten it. If it is flea dirt, it will turn a reddish-brown color because it contains blood.

If one household pet has fleas, you can safely assume that all of the pets in the household have them. Once infestation has occurred, elimination can be a maddening, frustrating, and expensive venture. More so than in most cases, prevention is therefore preferable to treatment. Preventing and treating flea and tick infestation will be discussed a little later in this chapter.

Ticks

There are many types of ticks, and each is a bloodsucker. Ticks are capable of spreading diseases to both animals and humans. Tick-borne diseases include Lyme disease, Rocky Mountain spotted fever, and ehrlichiosis.

Ticks don't jump or fly, but they can crawl for several feet. They attach to anything that gives off an odor of carbon dioxide, as humans and animals do. They make their home in cracks in the house, as well as outdoors—in all manner of things, including bushes, grass, weeds, woods, and brush.

Lyme Disease. Lyme disease was named for the town of Lyme, Connecticut, where the first human cases were diagnosed. Studies have shown that dogs from that area showed symptoms similar to those found in humans.

Animals and humans can get the disease from a variety of ticks—the small deer tick is by far the most common carrier of the disease. The symptoms in dogs include lethargy, lameness, joint pain, fever, and a loss of appetite. A vaccine is available for Lyme disease; discuss with your veterinarian whether it is appropriate for your dog. The veterinarians at Angell prefer to use a program of tick prevention unless there is a very high risk of exposure.

Rocky Mountain Spotted Fever. Another disease spread by ticks, Rocky Mountain spotted fever (RMSF), is seen primarily in the western United States and in New England. In the first (subclinical) stage, the dog will show no symptoms; in the second (acute) stage, the dog might experience loss of appetite, fever, joint and muscle pain, rash, or neurological problems like depression or dizziness. If RMSF is diagnosed early enough, antibiotics can treat it effectively and the dog will show improvement within the first twelve to twenty-four hours. Following recovery, the dog is probably immune to RMSF for up to twelve months—but reinfection can occur if the dog is exposed to the disease again.

Ehrlichiosis. This disease (pronounced "ear-lick-ee-osis"), transmitted by the brown dog tick, is becoming far more common. It is caused by organisms called *rickettsia* that are carried by the tick. Symptoms will appear within eight to twenty days after the bite of the infected tick. The disease has three phases: acute, subclinical, and chronic.

- During the *acute* phase, which lasts two to four weeks, the organisms enter certain cells in the dog and reproduce. Symptoms include fever, eye and nose discharge, anorexia, depression, lethargy, weight loss, and enlargement of the lymph glands. The dog may have mild anemia in the acute phase, which usually resolves by itself.
- The *subclinical* phase lasts forty to one hundred and twenty days. During this phase, either the dog will rid herself of the rickettsia or the disease will progress to the next phase.
- The *chronic* phase can last for years. The dog might suffer lethargy, loss of appetite, anemia, and neurological problems.

Ehrlichiosis is diagnosed by clinical signs and a blood test. Treatment includes antibiotics and supportive care.

Flea and Tick Prevention

Undertaking a program that will protect your pets from fleas and ticks requires thought, care, and work. Some products will kill either fleas or ticks, and some will kill both fleas and ticks and will help prevent them from attacking your dog. Talk with your veterinarian about the options that best suit you, your environment, and your pet.

If you have a very severe flea and tick infestation you may need to have your yard (or kennel) and home chemically treated. If you've hired a professional to do the task, ask the exterminator what the appropriate time of year is to treat the property.

Going over your pet in search of parasites should be part of daily grooming. In fact, thorough brushing and combing are an important part of parasite prevention, as is thorough vacuuming of your home and the dog's bedding. Give cracks and corners special attention. When you finish vacuuming, you'll have to either vacuum up some flea powder into your vacuum bag or throw the bag out. You don't want your vacuum cleaner to become an incubator for fleas, releasing more of the parasites into the environment as they hatch.

Tricks of the Trade

It is especially important to check for ticks after your dog has walked through tall grass or wooded areas, and for fleas whenever your dog is walked in grass. Be certain to do this before bringing the dog back into the house.

If you have more than one pet and one has fleas, you can assume that all of your pets have fleas. Finding one flea on your dog means that there are very likely hundreds of fleas, larva, pupa, and eggs in your house. Don't forget that the flea will spend the majority of its life in the environment, not on the dog, so these parasites may be difficult to locate. If your dog is scratching and you don't see any fleas on him, don't assume that one hasn't been there. It may well be in your house. And if you see tapeworm segments in your dog's stool, he may have had fleas and may still have them.

There are flea collars, shampoos, sprays, powders, and dips that are commercially available. The topical insecticide sprays, powders, and dips that were once so popular are giving way to the newer products since the effect of the older products is temporary. Flea life stages can persist for months, so chemicals with residual action are needed and should be repeated periodically. Sprays or foggers require that you leave the house for several hours while you're using them, which should be twice in two-week intervals and then every two months during flea season.

We're fortunate to be living in a time when there are new flea treatments available for pets that are more effective and environmentally friendly than anything we've had before. These new treatments actually help to control fleas. They are both oral and topical systemic treatments that not only treat the existing problem but serve to aid prevention as well.

Insect growth regulators (IGRs) control the fleas by killing flea larvae and eggs, thus interrupting their cycle of development. These products won't kill adult fleas, but they decrease the flea population by stopping their development. A common oral product is lufenuron. Given monthly, lufenuron is combined with heartworm prevention in a product called lufenuron/milbemycin. Lufenuron can also be given as an injection that lasts six months. Methoprene and pyriproxifen are also very effective insect growth regulators and those are available as sprays or collars.

There are products that kill the fleas (adulticides). These work very rapidly. They come as both spot-on and oral products. Spot-on products are usually applied to the skin between your dog's shoulders. The medication is then absorbed into the skin and distributed throughout the body. Fleas are quickly killed as soon as they make contact with the dog's skin. The spot-on products include fipronil, imadacloprid, and selemectin.

One of the newest products is nitenpyram, an oral adulticide that begins to kill fleas within thirty minutes.

When these new products are given correctly they are easy to use and the most effective methods of flea control. Some of them are also effective against other parasites. Some veterinarians will recommend a combination of an adulticide and an insect growth regulator to provide a more complete method of flea control.

As always with your wellness program, the choice of flea control will depend on your dog's lifestyle and the potential for exposure to these parasites. Working in conjunction with your veterinarian is key. Fortunately, these new monthly treatments can help reduce your dog's and her environment's parasites. If you live in an area with a high risk of fleas, keeping your pet on a monthly schedule of treatments is an excellent preventive method of controlling fleas.

Tricks of the Trade

Being watchful and immediately removing any ticks that you see is an important part of prevention. Avoid areas where ticks are known to reside. It is entirely possible that one will attach itself to your clothes and you will carry it to another location. If you've been in an area where there might be ticks, be certain to look carefully at your clothing and any exposed parts of your body before walking into your house.

If you live in an area at high risk for tick bites, such as the northeastern and midwestern United States, you will have to give some extra thought to where you walk your dog. Stay away from long uncut grass, low shrubs, or brush. Sand beaches are usually considered safe, as are pavement and closely mowed lawns. But be careful of very hot pavement, which can burn the pads of your dog's feet.

Before setting out on a walk, be certain to use the tick repellent that your veterinarian has prescribed. Follow the label directions carefully, as too much can be toxic to your pet. Keep pets indoors until the insecticide has dried.

Ticks vary from country to country. For example, a tick bite in Australia is taken very seriously because of the incidence of paralysis. Tick bites can cause some serious problems, including tick paralysis and encephalitis, so it's important to find and remove any ticks as rapidly as possible.

REMOVING TICKS FROM YOUR PET

When removing a tick, don't squeeze it or use nail polish, a hot match, or petroleum jelly. You may have heard these old wives' tales, but doing these things might cause infected material to be injected into the skin. Using tweezers, and preferably wearing gloves as a precaution against possible transmission of illness from the tick, hold the tweezers between the thumb and forefinger and grasp the tick as close to the skin as possible and pull it out slowly, straight up from the dog. There are tick removal devices on the market, or you may use a hemostat if you have one. If the head of the tick is still in the dog's skin, try to grab it with the tweezers and remove as much of it as you can. If you can't remove the entire head, don't worry. Your pet's immune system will create an inflammatory response at the area to try to dislodge the head. You can, however, call your veterinarian, who can use surgical instruments to remove the head of the tick if needed. It's also a good idea to isolate any new dogs and be certain there are no ticks on the dog before introducing her to the household and established pets.

Ticks may look like small dark specks of dirt on the dog's coat; if they're already attached to the dog and have begun sucking blood, the engorged tick can look like a small growth or a raisin. They are usually found around hairless areas such as the eyes and ears, so look carefully in these areas as well as the rest of the body and remove any ticks you find. If a tick is attached to your dog, time is of the essence: remove it as soon as possible.

There's an entire arsenal of new topical products on the market to prevent tick attachment and to detach ticks that attach to a dog. Tick collars do the same thing. In addition, you can kill ticks with special sprays, shampoos, dips, and powders. Topical drops, applied monthly to the skin, are most commonly used.

It should be noted that the presence of internal or external parasites can worsen any allergic condition, whether it's dermatological or gastrointestinal. An itchy dog is irritable, and an irritable dog can be itchy. Pruritus is neurochemically linked to anxiety, so veterinarians and veterinary behaviorists often treat anxious animals by first addressing their allergies.

What We've Learned

Alopecia: Hair loss; baldness

Anthelmintics: Medications that kill gastrointestinal parasites

Ascarids: A scientific term for roundworms

External parasites: Parasites that infest your dog's skin

Flea dirt: Small black specks that resemble pepper

Hot spots: Hairless spots that are red, raw, and weeping serum

Internal parasites: Parasites that are inside your dog

Microfilariae: Offspring of the adult heartworm

Pruritus: Intense itching

Pyoderma: Skin infection

Zoonotic: Referring to diseases that can spread between animals and people

3

A Little Maintenance

Many of the problems in this chapter cause
aggravation, irritation, and decreased vitality
to a very large number of pets. Don't settle for
anything less than beautiful, healthy skin and
hair coat and gleaming white teeth.
Both you and your pet will enjoy these
outward signs of good health.
— *Peter Theran, V.M.D.,*
Diplomate, A.C.V.I.M.

Regular grooming and dental care are important to your dog's
health. Daily brushing and combing are required for most dogs,
although the ones with an extremely short coat require less. Not
all dogs enjoy grooming, but it shouldn't be an unpleasant experience for
the dog and the owner. The key is to introduce it slowly in a positive environment. Once the dog knows what to expect and realizes that the owner
will be gentle, it can become a relaxing time for both.

Grooming is not only an opportunity to relax and bond with your dog,
but also a good time to check for parasites or possible skin problems. We'll

discuss some of the more common skin (dermatological) problems in this chapter.

Setting the Tone

Getting your dog accustomed to being touched will make grooming and medical exams more pleasant for everyone involved. Gently pass your hands over his body every day. Touch his ears and his feet. Brush the hair back from his nails and hold each nail to examine it. It's a good idea to put the clippers around the nail without cutting anything, so he'll get used to having this tool near his feet. Slip your finger into his mouth and touch his teeth. Talk softly and make this gentle touching part of your relaxation time together. All of these gentle touches are helping to prepare him for getting his nails trimmed, his ears examined and cleaned, and his teeth brushed.

It's unfortunate that many owners tend to wait to groom dogs who don't like it and then make a big production of grooming. This only makes matters worse, resulting in pain, struggle, and frustration. One way you can make this time more palatable for the dog is to put a glob of all-natural

GIVING PILLS

At some point you will likely need to give your dog a pill. This requires popping the pill into the back of the mouth, then closing the mouth and gently massaging the throat so he'll swallow. While there are pill "guns" available to pop the pill into the back of the mouth, it's so much easier on you and your dog if you can give a pill without this device. Pills may be hidden in a bit of soft cheese, but most dogs are intelligent enough to discover this little trick before long, learning to swallow the cheese and spit out the pill. But the better the treat, the less likely he will spit out the pill, especially if the pill is followed by another piece of the same special treat without a pill in it.

extra-chunky peanut butter on a cutting board, sit next to the dog, and work on grooming one small area while he's licking the peanut butter. (If your dog has pancreatitis or is predisposed to it, try using a low-fat flavored cream cheese in place of the peanut butter.) Repeat the process the next night. You will soon get your dog to overcome his concerns about grooming.

This is also a good time to practice medicating your dog so he'll find the experience familiar. Simply liquefy something tasty and put it in an oral dosing syringe (a syringe without a needle in it). Form a pocket at the side of his mouth between the cheek and gums and squirt the liquid into that area.

While you're practicing medicating your dog, this is also a good time to let him play with an ice cube—a good way of getting him to slowly consume water when he is ill. Letting him play with it now will make it familiar later when you really need it.

Start slowly and gently to get your dog accustomed to the process. You and your dog should feel comfortable and relaxed. If you're tense, your dog will feel tense as well. Dogs are skilled at reading body language and picking up on our cues even when we don't realize that we're sending messages. Relax and enjoy this time together. To discourage any wriggling or biting, praise your dog when he holds still. Give him a little treat when he's behaving well to further encourage good behavior. If you're clicker training (discussed further in Chapter 6, page 111), you can use the clicker to "mark" good behavior, such as when the dog or puppy lets you hold his foot, which is a prelude to cutting his nails. The click is followed by a treat, and the treat is accompanied by praise. Ultimately, the clicker is phased out (and the treat can be, too) but the praise remains. People like to hear that they're being good and doing something right, and dogs do, too.

Grooming

Grooming time is an ideal opportunity to check for any possible health problems, including parasites, and nip them in the bud before they blossom into bigger problems requiring more care. You may opt to take your dog to a professional groomer, or you may want to learn to do the grooming yourself. In either case you will still want to brush and comb your dog frequently if he has long hair, weekly if he has a very short coat.

If you've purchased your dog from a responsible breeder, the breeder will show you how to properly groom your new dog. There are also books and videos that can help you learn to groom properly. Your veterinarian can help you with some of the basics, such as checking ears, cutting nails, and brushing teeth. You could also ask your professional groomer which grooming schedule, equipment, and technique is right for your dog to keep him in good condition between professional grooming appointments.

Before his bath, brush and comb your dog thoroughly with a good-quality brush or comb (you should also have a good flea comb handy). Check his skin and coat carefully for any changes or possible problems. If he has a long coat, be certain that all tangles are removed before bathing. A little cornstarch worked into the hair and then brushed out can aid in

GOOD GROOMING MEANS GOOD HEALTH

Grooming is a very important part of your pet's health program, although it's commonly overlooked. Routine brushing and combing removes dead hair and dirt, prevents mats, and reduces hairball formation. Because it stimulates the blood supply to the skin, grooming gives your pet a healthier and shinier coat.

Start regular grooming when you bring your pet home and make it a part of your pet's daily routine. Purchase a good-quality brush and comb. Start slowly. Get your puppy used to being handled by making it a pleasant and positive experience. Praise him when he holds still. Discourage wriggling and biting. Soon your pet will come to enjoy this time and extra attention. Some dogs may have special grooming needs and require special equipment. Your veterinarian, breeder, or professional groomer can advise you.

Bathing needs vary greatly for each animal. A good rule of thumb is to bathe your pet only when he needs it—such as when the coat becomes dirty or odorous. If there are persistent problems with scratching or flaky skin, your pet may need a removing tangles, but mats will probably have to be carefully cut or clipped out, and that will require an experienced groomer so the dog's skin isn't cut in the process.

Bathe your dog whenever he is dirty or begins to have an odor. Show dogs are bathed weekly, but there's no need to bathe a pet that frequently unless he's very dirty.

It's a good idea to put a lubricating eye ointment (which can be bought over the counter) in his eyes before you begin to bathe your dog, and place cotton in his ears so water doesn't get in his ear canal. Ask your veterinarian or professional groomer to show you how to gently use a bit of ear cleaner on a cotton ball to clean his ears. Dogs can develop an infection as a result of moisture in the ear canal—especially dogs whose ears flop over, providing a warm, moist haven in which yeast or bacteria thrive. Don't use cotton swabs to clean your dog's ears, as this could damage his ear canal. Even if you see your veterinarian using them, don't try it yourself.

---

special shampoo or have a skin problem that your veterinarian should examine. Skin problems—including fleas, ticks, allergies, and infections—are common among dogs. Most conditions are manageable with early detection and treatment. Routine grooming can help. Pay attention to any potential problems. If you notice excessive scratching, hair loss, or flaky skin, contact your veterinarian.

Grooming is also a good time to check your pet's nails and trim them before they become too long or sharp. While clipping nails is a painless and simple process, it does take some patience in the beginning. Your veterinarian or technician should teach you the proper method. A specially designed pet nail clipper will help, as will starting at a young age and establishing a routine.

Get your pet used to having his paws handled before you attempt to use the clippers, then start slowly. Even if you can clip only a few nails in one sitting before your pet's patience runs out, you are on the right track. Maintain a regular schedule and be persistent. Your pet will eventually learn to cooperate.

From the Animal Wellness Program at Angell Memorial Animal Hospital

If his ears have any kind of abnormal discharge or are inflamed, take him to your veterinarian.

Place a nonskid liner in the tub or in the sink. The water should be warm, not hot. Your dog should learn that a bath can be a relaxing experience. Be sure that your hands are supportive so he doesn't feel as if he's going to slip, and talk to him using a soft, encouraging tone of voice. Think of a dog's bath as being like a shower: rinse thoroughly. And if the dog has a long coat, be careful not to rub the hair together or you'll create a huge mat.

Where you begin washing will depend on your dog. If your dog has a pushed-in face (that is, he is *brachycephalic*), do the head last and use a washcloth to gently wash the head. You don't want to interfere with the dog's ability to breathe, so do this as gently as possible. Wash the head last if your dog doesn't like having his head washed—this way you can take him right out of the bath after his head has been rinsed off. Consider bathing the head first if the dog has fleas because the fleas may go to the head if you save that for last. Try to prevent the fleas from going to your dog's eyes and ears. Don't forget to wash his muzzle when you wash his head.

Shampoo may be followed by a coat conditioner specifically formulated for dogs. Be sure to rinse both out well. Conditioner is especially important if your dog receives frequent baths or if his hair is long and likely to tangle. It's important to use a shampoo formulated especially for dogs because their pH is different from that of a human. A wide variety of canine shampoos and conditioners are on the market. You might want to choose one based on his coat type, and keep in mind that a hypoallergenic shampoo may be best. You can use a tearless shampoo for puppies and adults. This would also be a good choice if your dog squirms in the bath and you're afraid of getting shampoo in his eyes. Discuss with your veterinarian which products are best for your dog.

Gently wrap your dog in a towel to absorb excess moisture. Next, blow his coat dry using an electric hair dryer on a warm setting. Be careful to move the dryer around to avoid burning your dog's delicate skin—don't let the dryer stay too long on one spot. Be sure to brush through the hair as you blow dry so that you won't cause tangles. Many dogs enjoy this part of the process and will lie on their side, completely relaxed, while being brushed.

Cutting Nails

Some dogs spend enough time running on pavement or gravel to wear down their nails, but many more will need their nails trimmed. If you're not comfortable doing it, have it done by your veterinarian or a professional groomer. Either can show you how to properly cut your dog's nails so as to avoid the blood vessel inside the nail that is commonly called the *quick*. It's a simple procedure that requires a nail clipper designed especially for dogs.

It does necessitate patience, especially in the beginning. If you start when your dog is young, you can establish a routine. Holding his feet daily in a nonthreatening way will make it easier to begin trimming his nails. Start slowly. There's no need to rush and no need to feel tense. And you don't have to do all of his nails at one time; you can do a few at a time. Trim just a little at a time at first.

Look for the pink area at the middle of the nail; this is the quick that you need to avoid. Many people whose dogs have black nails prefer to have it done by a professional since it's hard to see the quick in a black nail. If your dog has black nails, get a good small halogen flashlight (like the ones used by campers), hold the nail, turn the flashlight on, and aim from under the nail. Draw a ring with a thick marker pen around the far margin of the vein, which you can now see. Cut away from the pen mark. Keep some styptic powder or cornstarch nearby to stop any bleeding in case you accidentally cut the quick.

Some dogs do best if you clip their nails while they're standing. If you use the non-guillotine clippers you can get him to stand and cut the nails while pressing the feet to the ground.

Don't forget to trim the nail on the dewclaws if your dog has dewclaws. A dewclaw is like an extra toe on the side of the foot. If your dog has floppy dewclaws that might get caught on something, your veterinarian may suggest removing them for the dog's safety and comfort.

If you allow the nails to grow too long, the quick will grow longer as well. In the worst-case scenario, if the nails aren't trimmed they can grow around and under the foot, into the paw pad.

Be sure to reward your dog with praise, and perhaps a treat, when he cooperates. But don't overdo the food rewards because you don't want to create a weight problem.

Dental Care

Puppies have twenty-eight teeth, while adult dogs have forty-two permanent teeth: twenty in the maxilla (upper jaw) and twenty-two in the mandible (lower jaw). Brushing your dog's teeth should become part of your daily routine. Begin by getting your puppy or dog accustomed to having your fingers in his mouth. (This will also make it easier when your veterinarian needs to examine your dog's teeth.)

If your dog is reluctant to let you put your finger in her mouth, try wrapping a small washcloth around your finger, putting a dab of doggy toothpaste on it, and letting your dog lick it. Or just put a little of the toothpaste on your finger. Gently move the washcloth or your finger to the dog's mouth and move it gently around his teeth and gums. Brush in small circles along gumlines, moving from the back to the front of the mouth. It's OK if he swallows the toothpaste—that's why you're using a specially designed dog toothpaste, because it won't harm him. Dirty teeth, however, *are* harmful. The bacteria from around diseased teeth and gums can get into the bloodstream and may cause a variety of health problems, including those that can affect the liver, heart, or kidneys.

You may either use a specially designed doggy toothbrush or a soft-bristled toothbrush made for humans. Fingertip brushes are not recommended because their little rubber nubbins cannot get below the gumline to sweep away plaque the way bristles can. It is the mechanical removal of plaque on a daily basis that is the benefit of brushing.

Your dog will learn to open his mouth for you when he sees the toothbrush if you pair treats with the requests. Say "Open," give him a treat, brush his teeth, and then give him another treat. This practice may also help you notice the development of behavior problems. If your dog is older than a year and begins growling when you brush his teeth, when he has previously tolerated brushing, he has a dental problem or is developing an aggression. In either case, you have just spotted it early when it's easily treated. Brushing your dog's teeth is very valuable for his health, so keep at it. Even if you manage to brush only the outside of the upper teeth, you will be accomplishing something.

Tricks of the Trade

The key to brushing is to get the bristles of the brush along the gumlines of the outside of the upper teeth—no fingers are necessary. This way, the mouth can be opened or closed, whatever is comfortable and least restraining for the dog. It's important to keep things simple and efficient; this increases the chances that you'll persist in the practice and do it correctly, whether it's brushing teeth or any other pet care procedure.

Brushing your dog's teeth daily is a habit you should maintain for your dog's lifetime. Twice a day is excellent, but once a day is sufficient. Your dog will still need periodic professional cleanings to remove plaque and tartar and polish the teeth. Don't mistake scraping tartar off the teeth for a cure-all; it may damage the enamel and the gums. It's important for the dog to have appropriate cleanings, which include scaling and polishing while under anesthesia. A proper scaling and polishing will clean the teeth below the gumline.

Brushing your dog's teeth at home, along with appropriate professional cleanings, may help eliminate or decrease the need for dental procedures later on. This is far preferable to having tooth extractions and other dental surgeries. It's important to note that once the gumline recedes, that cannot be reversed.

Toy breeds will often retain their baby teeth. Small dogs tend to have crowding because they have the same number of teeth as larger dogs and the teeth are fairly large relative to their mouth size. This crowding can increase the likelihood of plaque and tartar accumulation and may also

A TOOTH FOR A TOOTH

PROPER DENTAL CARE AND YOUR PET'S HEALTH

Most dog owners don't realize that dental disease is one of the most common problems affecting pets.

Often beginning at a very young age, food particles, bacteria, and debris build up at the gumline and under the gums to form plaque. Once plaque hardens (calcifies) to become calculus, dental scaling and polishing by a veterinary technician or veterinarian is needed. If plaque is allowed to accumulate unchecked it causes a variety of dental conditions, from mild discomfort and bad breath to receding gums, tooth-root abscesses, and loss of teeth. Bacteria associated with tooth and gum disease can spread to internal body organs and cause systemic infections.

By providing routine dental care at home you can delay, or even prevent, dental disease—and keep your pet's teeth clean and healthy.

Getting Started

Routine home dental care should start when your pet is about three months old. Ideally, you should brush teeth once daily. However, brushing at least three times each week will go a long way in helping prevent dental and related health problems.

Start slowly by lifting up the lip and running your finger or a damp washcloth wrapped around your finger along the gums and teeth. Talk to and praise your pet to keep him calm while you are doing this. Gradually increase the amount of time you work in the mouth daily. Concentrate on the outside surface of the teeth. Very affect the alignment of the dog's teeth. The rule of thumb is that there should never be two teeth in the same space at the same time. Your veterinarian will want to extract any baby teeth that are still present at the time the adult teeth are coming into their proper place.

Greyhounds are more prone to periodontal disease than most other dogs, as are dogs with compromised immune systems.

---

little periodontal disease develops on the inside surface of the teeth since the tongue keeps this area clean.

Establish a Routine
The best time to clean you pet's teeth is after the evening meal. Your pet will become more cooperative over time if you establish a routine. For example: first feed your pet, next clean the teeth, then play with your dog or take him for a walk. Most pets adapt to this routine surprisingly well.

What You'll Need
You can use a soft toothbrush or a moist washcloth wrapped around your finger. A child's toothbrush or specific veterinary products are ideal. The rubbing or brushing motion against the teeth is what produces the results. Toothpaste specifically formulated for pets is recommended. Baking soda toothpaste may also be used, but the taste of human toothpaste is objectionable to most pets and can cause indigestion if swallowed.

The Technique
Use the toothbrush or washcloth in a circular motion, concentrating on the gum line on the outside of the teeth. There may be some minor bleeding when you first start; however, this stops as the gums become healthier. After cleaning, rinse the mouth with a squirt bottle or allow your pet to drink water.

Remember
Starting at a young age and establishing a good routine will help make dental care a positive experience for both you and your pet, and help prevent illness and discomfort.

From the Animal Wellness Program at Angell Memorial Animal Hospital

Bad breath (*halitosis*) is often a sign of infection. If your dog's breath begins to smell despite regular brushing, be sure to get him to the veterinarian to have his teeth and gums checked. Other signs to watch for are lip smacking and salivation, which are indicative of oral pain. If your dog is drooling and that's not considered normal for your dog (St. Bernards and Newfoundlands, for example, usually drool), call your veterinarian and schedule an appointment. Other signs of dental disease are decreased appetite, a change in food preference from dry to wet, decreased recreational chewing, oral bleeding, and lethargy. That older dog might not be lethargic simply because he's old, but because he is experiencing mouth pain—and a cleaning can make him feel like a young dog once again.

Orthodontic diseases occur when either the mandible (lower jaw) or the maxilla (upper jaw) is too long or too short, or when one or more teeth are out of alignment. In some breeds, such as the Shih Tzu, the elongated lower jaw (*prognathism*) is considered normal. Dog breeders refer to this condition as an *undershot bite*. When the owner learns this term, the owner and the veterinarian can find themselves talking about two different things since the veterinarian will think that the owner means that the upper jaw is protruding while the owner means exactly the opposite. This could cause some confusion.

Feeding dry food will help your dog clean his own teeth as chewing releases saliva. Your dog will also appreciate clean, fresh water to drink. Not only is water healthy to drink, it also helps the dog "rinse" after eating or having his teeth brushed.

Safe chewtoys are also important to help clean the teeth. Safe chewables include dry snacks; ropes (but those can be torn to pieces and swallowed, possibly causing an obstruction, so be sure to watch while your dog is playing with them and put them out of reach when you're not available to monitor playtime); toys that are hollow at one end so you can place a biscuit inside or coat the inside with peanut butter or doggy toothpaste to keep your dog or puppy busy; and rawhides (which also need to be watched carefully). Inappropriate chewables include bones, hooves (they can break teeth), hard toys that resemble bones, and rocks. Any of these items can cause a fractured tooth, which could lead to an abscess.

Dogs, like humans, can get cavities and periodontal disease. Taking care of your dog's teeth prevents problems later on. Don't ignore this important part of your dog's wellness program.

Dermatological Problems

If your dog licks or scratches frequently or is losing hair, he might have a dermatological problem. If you notice these symptoms, make an appointment with your veterinarian to have your dog evaluated as soon as possible. The earlier a diagnosis is made, the sooner treatment can begin.

Skin problems, like parasite infestations, allergies, and infections, are common and require veterinary attention. If they become more complicated, your veterinarian may refer you to a board-certified veterinary dermatologist. Dermatologists are also allergists, so any allergy problems will be referred to the dermatologist as well. The dermatologist's job is rather like detective work, trying to determine the root cause of the problem and then resolve it. This process requires patience and vigilance from the owner, who must observe and report to the doctor any changes in the dog's environment and symptoms that might facilitate a diagnosis. Each dermatological and allergic problem will have different treatment options.

Let's consider some of the more common dermatological conditions your dog might encounter.

Ringworm

Ringworm, also known as *dermatophytosis*, is actually a fungal infection. It acquired the name *ringworm* long ago when it was thought to be a worm living under the skin that caused circular lesions in the skin of humans who had the disease. The infection can occur in the hair, superficial layer of the skin, or nail. It is less common in dogs than it is in cats. It occurs when the outer layer of skin is damaged and hair follicles become vulnerable to infection. The infection causes the hair shafts to become fragile, enabling them to break off and contaminate the environment.

Tricks of the Trade

Discuss your environment with your veterinarian so you can work out a program to end ringworm and prevent it from recurring or being transmitted to anyone else in the household.

Ringworm is more likely to occur in young dogs with incompletely developed immune systems or older dogs whose immune systems are compromised by diseases or drug treatment. It is a zoonotic disease and is spread by contact with infected hair or scales on other animals, in the environment, or on grooming equipment. A dermatophyte culture is the most reliable diagnostic test.

The disease may resolve itself in time, but treatment is advisable to shorten the duration of the infection and reduce contagion to other animals and people. Newer drugs are being used to treat ringworm that are safer and more effective than some of the older treatments. There is a vaccine that may be used together with drug therapy. Specific treatment will depend on a variety of factors, including the extent of the infection and your dog's overall age and health. Discuss your options with your veterinarian. A negative culture should be obtained before therapy is discontinued.

Otitis Externa

Otitis externa is an inflammation of the external ear canal. Floppy ears, excessive moisture in the ears, or trauma from cotton swabs can predispose dogs to this problem. Among the breeds prone to otitis externa are German Shepherds, Labrador Retrievers, Golden Retrievers, and both Cocker and Springer Spaniels. A secondary bacterial or yeast infection may develop. If your dog has recurrent ear infections, you and your veterinarian need to identify the underlying cause. Primary causes include mites, allergies, foreign bodies, and autoimmune diseases. Something is fueling the infection and keeping it going.

Keeping the ears clean will help. Have your veterinarian show you the proper way to clean your dog's ears. Your veterinarian will also help you decide whether the hair should be pulled from the ear canal as part of grooming. If your veterinarian determines that it should be removed, then either the veterinarian or a professional groomer is the best person to do it, though they can show you how to remove the hair properly if you decide that you want to do it yourself.

Acute Moist Dermatitis

Commonly known as *hot spots*, acute moist dermatitis is caused by very itchy (*pruritic*) skin conditions. Once the dog starts licking and biting an itchy area, hot spots may appear, often around the rump or on the side of the face. Flea allergy is the most common cause, but other allergies, other parasites, irritant substances, anal sac disease, and ear problems can also be underlying causes. It's not age related, and is more common in breeds with dense coats, such as Golden Retrievers and St. Bernards.

Treatment begins with clipping and cleaning the affected area and varies according to the severity of the lesion. The goal is to break the itch–lick cycle. Topical treatments will be given, with or without a systemic treatment. Topical drying agents, antibiotics, or steroids may be given. Oral cortisone drugs may be prescribed. True hot spots are not skin infections, but in some cases the dermatitis extends deeper than the skin surface and systemic antibiotics are needed.

Being aware of your dog's scratching and getting him to the veterinarian for early diagnosis will go a long way in breaking the self-perpetuating cycle. It's important to try to identify the underlying cause and treat it so the hot spots are not recurrent.

Irritant Contact Dermatitis

Primary irritant contact dermatitis causes an inflammation when a dog's skin is directly exposed to a substance that irritates it. Intensity of symptoms and quickness of onset will depend on the nature and quantity of the irritant, as well as the length of contact with the dog's skin. For example, strong acids or alkalies will immediately injure the skin. Severe reactions to such substances are chemical burns. Weaker substances need prolonged or repeated exposure to cause a reaction in the dog. Soaps, detergents, topical medications, weed and insecticide sprays, carpet cleaners, and disinfectants are among these substances.

A dog with irritant contact dermatitis might have red patches and little bumps on the skin. Crusts can develop. Intense itchiness can result in severe scratching and biting. If the cause isn't immediately apparent, you will need to give your veterinarian a detailed history in order to discover what has caused the contact dermatitis. When the cause can't be found, treatment will include systemic and topical medications, as well as bathing the irritated areas with a very mild, nonirritating shampoo.

Superficial Bacterial Folliculitis

This condition is an infection of the hair follicles and in most cases is caused by a staphylococcal bacterium. Underlying predisposing factors include local trauma, allergies, parasites, and hormonal disorders. A variety of lesions may be seen: red bumps (*papules*), pimples (*pustules*), crusts, and hair loss. The degree of itchiness varies from nonexistent to intense.

Diagnosis is made via clinical appearance, microscopic study of cells (*cytology*), culture, and, in some cases, biopsy. Treatment includes systemic antibiotics, typically for twenty-one days. If the infection recurs, it is important to try to identify an underlying disorder.

Malassezia Dermatitis

Malassezia is a yeast that normally inhabits a dog's skin and ears but can cause an itchy dermatitis in some dogs if it proliferates. Commonly affected areas include the ears, lips, front of the neck, armpits, groin, and paws. The skin may be greasy and scaly, and there may be an odor. Predisposed breeds include West Highland White Terriers, Basset Hounds, Shih Tzu, and American Cocker Spaniels.

Diagnosis is usually made via cytology. If the condition is widespread, treatment with an oral antifungal in conjunction with topical treatment will be most effective. In many cases, there is an underlying predisposing disorder such as an allergy or hormonal condition.

Urticaria and Angioedema

Urticaria is commonly known as *hives*, and the lesions in this condition are called *wheals*. Angioedema refers to a large swelling caused by fluid. It is often localized to the head, especially the muzzle and eyelids. These conditions may or may not be itchy. Causes of these disorders include drugs, vaccines, foods, and stinging and biting insects. Treatment depends on the severity of the condition and may include antihistamines, steroids, and epinephrine.

Canine Atopy

Canine atopic dermatitis, or canine atopy, presents with itching that often involves the face, feet, ears, and underside. Dogs with this condition can commonly develop secondary bacterial and/or *Malassezia* yeast infections. This disorder is considered a hypersensitivity to inhaled or percutaneously absorbed environmental substances (allergens) in genetically predisposed dogs.

Atopy is common, and the most typical age of onset is between one and three years of age. The dog's scratching may lead to spots that are red and seeping, as well as rashes and hair loss. Predisposed breeds include Golden and Labrador Retrievers, Shar-Peis, Terriers, Dalmations, Lhasa Apsos, Shih Tzu, Cocker Spaniels, and English Setters.

To reach a diagnosis your veterinarian will need to take a thorough history and perform a full examination. Skin scrapings, a diet trial, and allergy testing may also help the veterinarian diagnose your pet.

If your pet is allergic to dust mites, molds, or pollens you'll need to start a prevention program. Mattress covers on bedding can help with dust mite allergy. Every week, wash in hot water any bedding that your dog lies on.

Keeping your dog off overstuffed furniture is ideal, but if you want him to have access to the furniture you can cover it in plastic. Dogs with allergies are better off without stuffed toys, which provide a haven for dust mites. Clean all of the dog's toys—especially the stuffed ones, if he can't be parted from them. Don't let him sleep with his toys. Keep your dog out of places where dust might settle—for example, under the bed. Vacuuming is a good preventive but it stirs up dust, so keep him out of the area while you vacuum and for an hour after vacuuming. Of course, not having rugs would be optimal. Both a dehumidifier and a HEPA filter may be helpful.

Options for treatment include those that address symptoms like itching (antihistamines, fatty acids, steroids) and immunotherapy (allergy injections).

Pemphigus Foliaceus

Pemphigus foliaceus is an autoimmune skin disease that produces scaling skin, scabbiness, and pustules. At early onset the disease may be confined to the head, but later it spreads to more of the body. Careful examination of the skin may reveal the presence of pustules, though they rupture quickly and may not be seen. Severely affected dogs may have fever and malaise. Akitas and Chows are predisposed to pemphigus foliaceus.

STEROIDS

Your dog may be prescribed a corticosteroid for short-term relief of itching. These drugs work by reducing inflammation and therefore relieving itching. They are often very effective, but long-term treatment should be avoided. Because steroids can have serious side effects, they are a treatment of last resort. If your dog takes steroids, be vigilant about keeping his bowl full of fresh water, as the drugs often cause increased thirst.

Diagnosis is made via biopsy and culture. Treatment usually consists of high doses of steroids with or without other immunosuppressive drugs. Antibiotics and topical therapy may also be prescribed. Dogs must be monitored very carefully for drug side effects. Although the medication is tapered gradually, most dogs with pemphigus foliaceus remain on a low dose of medication throughout their lifetime.

Discoid Lupus Erythematosus (DLE)

DLE is an immune-mediated skin disease. Symptoms are mostly confined to the nose area and include loss of pigment, redness, scaling, crusting, and sores. The lesions may spread up the bridge of the nose with time. Similar lesions may be seen on the lips, around the eyes, and on the ears. Predisposed breeds include Collies, Shetland Sheepdogs, German Shepherds, and Siberian Huskies. Diagnosis is made via skin biopsy. Therapy will vary depending on the severity of the disease. Mild cases may be treated with oral vitamin E, oral fatty acid supplementation, and topical steroids. Other oral medication may be prescribed in severe cases. All dogs with DLE should avoid direct sunlight; be sure to apply sunscreen to the dog when he does need to be outside.

Skinfold Dermatitis

Skinfold dermatitis is the general term for skin infections that occur secondary to skin that folds over itself, leaving an environment for moisture to accumulate, macerating the skin and leaving it vulnerable for infection.

Dogs with large flaps at the lip, such as the Cocker and Springer Spaniels and the St. Bernard, can develop lipfold dermatitis. With lipfold, the odor and the chronic wetness of the skin just below the lower lip on the side of the face is what the owner will smell and see, respectively. With other skinfold infections, the most common signs are inflamed skin and licking or rubbing at the area.

In brachycephalic breeds such as the English Bulldog and Pekingese, as well as dogs with skinfolds like the Shar-Pei, the face is likely to be affected. Brachycephalic dogs with corkscrew tails, such as the Pug and Boston Terrier, can develop tailfold dermatitis. The skin under the tail becomes softened by the moisture that results from the folds, and it can become reddened and develop a bad odor.

Bodyfold dermatitis can be seen in the Shar-Pei, Basset Hound, Dachshund, and obese dogs. It causes redness and seborrhea and can emit a bad odor. Sometimes the body- or legfolds become itchy. Vulvar fold dermatitis develops in the folds of obese females or those with a small, recessed vulva. The skin becomes red and moist, and the folds can emit a terrible odor. Other symptoms include excessive vulvar licking and painful urination. The dog may also have a urinary tract infection.

If the cause of skinfold dermatitis is obesity, the dog will be placed on a weight reduction program. The excess skinfolds can be removed surgically in the case of face, lip, or vulvar folds, or the tail can be amputated. Surgery cures the problem. The alternative to surgery is long-term topical therapy. Concurrent diseases, such as gingivitis, dental disease, corneal ulcers, or urinary tract infections, must also be treated. It's best to consult your veterinarian about specific treatments for your dog.

Acral Lick Dermatitis

This condition, also known as *lick granuloma*, results when the dog licks or chews a spot on his leg repeatedly, causing a skin lesion to form. The area the dog licks or chews can become inflamed or even ulcerated. The licking may be in response to itchiness or pain, but it may be a behavioral problem. The underlying cause could be allergies, demodicosis, reaction to a foreign body, trauma, bacterial or fungal infection, hypothyroidism, osteopathy, or neuropathy. A secondary infection may also be present, which should be treated with systemic antibiotics for six to eight weeks and continued for two weeks beyond the time that the infection is gone. The underlying cause must be identified and corrected. Acral lick dermatitis is most common in Doberman Pinschers, Golden Retrievers and Labrador Retrievers, Great Danes, German Shepherds, and Irish Setters.

Topical medication may help stop the itchiness. Your veterinarian might recommend that the dog wear an Elizabethan collar or a bandage so that he can't get at the spot to continue licking; but note that bandages can act as a focus for licking and make the problem worse. If the root cause is obsessive-compulsive disorder, the dog will need behavioral therapy, which may be accompanied by medication such as fluoxetine or amitriptyline.

Other Conditions

Here are some other conditions your dog might develop.

Impacted Anal Sacs

Anal sacs are structures on either side of the anus that may overfill and become impacted or infected. The sacs can be emptied (expressed) by your veterinarian or groomer, who can show you how to do it yourself. One very obvious symptom of impacted anal sacs is "scooting" across the floor—that is, the dog drags his rear end as if trying to scratch it or relieve pressure or discomfort. Anal sacs may be removed surgically if the problem becomes severe.

Hypothyroidism

This disease is characterized by a deficiency of thyroid hormone. It's usually the result of destruction or atrophy of the thyroid gland. This condition usually occurs in middle-aged to older dogs, though it can be seen earlier in the large and Giant breeds. Congenital hypothyroidism is rare and results in dwarfism.

Hypothyroidism may affect any breed. Predisposed breeds include Old English Sheepdogs, Golden Retrievers, Doberman Pinschers, Chows, Cocker Spaniels, Irish Setters, Miniature Schnauzers, Dachshunds, and Airedales.

Symptoms include hair loss, changes in coat quality, increased skin pigment, thickening of the skin, scaling, secondary infections, lethargy, weight gain, neuromuscular disorders, and reproductive problems.

Diagnosis is made via blood test. Treatment consists of oral thyroid hormone supplementation given once or twice daily, and is continued for life. This is a complex issue best discussed with your veterinarian.

For more on hypothyroidism, see Chapters 9 and 10.

What We've Learned

Alopecia: Hair loss
Cytology: The microscopic study of cells
Halitosis: Bad breath
Mandible: Lower jaw
Maxilla: Upper jaw
Necrosis: The morphological changes that indicate the death of cells
Papules: Red bumps on the skin
Prognathism: An elongated lower jaw
Pruritic: Itchy
Pustules: Pimples
Quick: Blood vessel inside the nail

4

All the Comforts of Home

This chapter could be titled, "Be Prepared."
Read it at least two weeks before your pet arrives
so you can utilize all this practical advice.
— Peter Theran, V.M.D.,
Diplomate, A.C.V.I.M.

Just as you would prepare your home for the arrival of a new baby, you'll want to prepare it for the arrival of your new dog. Rather than running out at the last minute buying things that may be inappropriate, the time to buy the basics is before you bring the newcomer home. Take your time shopping for suitable equipment and toys with an eye toward safety and comfort. We'll start with the necessities and then discuss a few of the nonessentials that might be useful.

Crate

A dog crate is a useful housetraining tool and a safe place for your dog. However, it should not be used as a punishment. (Crate training and other techniques will be discussed in Chapter 6.) Be sure to buy a crate that's sturdy and has ample ventilation. You'll have a choice of fiberglass, wire, or stainless steel. (A fabric carrier is an option for road travel.) Each type of crate is suited to travel, although the fiberglass crates and some wire crates are the ones approved for airline use.

Some of the wire crates fold for easy carrying and storage. However, be certain that the wires aren't so far apart that the dog can get her tag, collar, paw, or anything else caught. And take care that the opening between the bottom of the crate and the pan isn't so large that the dog can get trapped in it.

Tricks of the Trade

If you choose a lightweight fiberglass crate, it should be secured with a seat belt for car travel to ensure that it doesn't fly off the seat if you have to stop quickly.

The crate should have a secure latch on the door, but you should also be able to open it easily with one hand without fumbling. Most crates have the door at one end, while some have it on the side—the choice is purely personal and is often dictated by the way the crate is placed in the car. For example, some people who drive a station wagon prefer the side opening.

You should purchase a crate pad for your dog's comfort. During the housetraining process, however, you will be better off lining the crate with newspapers and covering those with a soft, fluffy towel that can be easily washed if the puppy has an accident.

The crate will probably come equipped with a water dish that hitches onto the door, although some people prefer to train their dog to use a water bottle that can be licked (the type commonly used for rabbits), which will avoid spillage.

Baby Gates

While you're introducing your new puppy to the house and housetraining her, it's best to confine her to one room. This is not only helpful during the housetraining process, but safer for the puppy—the fewer rooms she can explore, the less trouble she can get into. You can purchase a baby gate to confine the puppy. Choose a gate with your puppy's size in mind—if you have a very small dog, she can be injured if the openings in the gate are too large. The gate should also fit securely so it doesn't fall over on the puppy when she inevitably stands up and holds on to it or runs into it.

Gates have a variety of openings, and some are made to conform to oddly shaped doorways. In this respect, preference and need will help you decide which gate to purchase.

Tricks of the Trade

Some dogs feel trapped by gates and crates. You should not use gates and crates if your dog is like this, or she could develop a panic disorder. Either keep the dog in one room with a door that can be closed securely, or keep her on a long lead that is attached to you in some fashion (for example, tied to your belt).

Dishes

Food and water dishes come in a variety of sizes and materials. Choosing the appropriate size isn't difficult. Smaller sizes are appropriate for smaller dogs; larger ones are right for larger dogs. If you've purchased your dog from a responsible breeder, ask what sort of dishes they use so your new pet will be using something familiar.

Stainless steel dishes are popular because they're easily cleaned. Some dogs have an allergic reaction to plastic dishes. Ceramic dishes should be checked to ensure that they don't contain lead.

Some owners opt for a feeding station—a holder containing water and food dishes that can be easily removed for filling and cleaning. Some of the stations are elevated. Some dishes are weighted so the dog can't tip them over and spill the contents. A nonskid placemat is optional, but may keep messes to a minimum and help prevent your dog from playing with her dishes.

Collars and Leashes

There are many types of collars, but a simple fabric collar with a buckle is a good investment. It should be wide and flat. You should be able to comfortably fit two fingers side by side under the collar. You don't want it too

SUPPLY CHECKLIST

Here are the basic supplies you'll need for your new dog:

- Crate
- Baby gate
- Dishes for food and water
- Collar or harness
- Leash
- Nail trimmer
- Brush and comb
- Shampoo and conditioner
- Deodorizer
- Toys
- Books and videos

tight, and you don't want it so loose that the dog can slip it off. Check the collar periodically to make sure it is still fitting comfortably, especially if you have a puppy. People sometimes forget that puppies grow rapidly, and their neck circumference can outgrow a collar in a short period of time. Some collars glow in the dark, which is a nice safety feature.

Dogs with a long, narrow muzzle, such as the Italian Greyhound, Greyhound, Saluki, and Afghan Hound, may do better with a *Martingale collar*, which has one solid side but does tighten to prevent the dog from slipping the collar.

You'll find that there are many collars on the market that are designed to allow you to inflict harm (pain) on the dog as a means of punishment and training. These include choke collars, prong collars, electronic collars, and other negative training tools. These kinds of collars are never appropriate; positive training is simple and doesn't take very long. (We'll talk about positive training in Chapter 6.)

A harness is a great choice for a dog who has a collapsing trachea or is predisposed to that condition, such as the Miniature Poodle and virtually all of the toy breeds, because the harness won't put any pressure on that area. Harnesses can also be helpful for dogs with neck problems like cervical instability, such as Doberman Pinschers. Harnesses are best for little dogs unless you're trying to teach your dog to pull something (like a sled), because a dog's natural response is to push back against pressure.

Leashes, sometimes called *leads*, come in a variety of sizes and colors. Many collars and leashes are made to match and can be very attractive. The leash should be made of leather or a sturdy fabric, not chains. Six feet is the average length of a leash, although they come in other sizes for other purposes. An average-length leash is all the pet owner usually needs. Much longer leashes are often used during training classes; your instructor will recommend the appropriate length.

Some owners like to use a *retractable leash*, which allows the dog more leeway to explore on country walks while still under the owner's control. A *show lead* is a one-piece leash and collar with an adjustable metal clasp. While it's good for the show ring, it isn't practical away from dog shows since it doesn't have a place for tags.

Nail Trimmers

Nail trimmers come in different styles and sizes to suit you and your dog. Don't use nail trimmers made for humans because they can split the nail and harm the quick. Some nail clippers are designed for large dogs, while others are for smaller dogs.

Tricks of the Trade

After her bath, when the dog is still in the tub, her nails will be softer and easier to cut, and she'll be more receptive to having her nails cut. Get your dog accustomed to baths and to nail trims the same way—slowly and surely. Keep the experience positive!

Nail trimmers are of two basic designs. One resembles scissors in its trimming action, using two blades. This style comes in several choices, including one that has a safety lock and safety stop bar to keep the nail at a safe cutting distance. The other, called a *guillotine*, has an elongated area into which you place the nail; you then squeeze the handles together, which lowers the single blade and trims the nail. The guillotine style is often chosen by beginners. Your choice is a matter of personal preference; your veterinarian or groomer can help you.

While you're purchasing your nail trimmer, don't forget to buy some styptic powder, which you'll need in order to stop any bleeding if you accidentally nick the blood vessel inside the nail. (You can alternatively use cornstarch.) It's easy to cut the quick with black nails, because you cannot see it as easily as with white nails.

Brushes

While you may choose to let your professional groomer take care of trimming your dog's nails, you will definitely need to buy a brush and comb.

Grooming is important and shouldn't be ignored. If you've purchased your dog from a responsible breeder, he can advise you on the best type of brush and comb to use on that breed's coat type.

Tricks of the Trade

When brushing your dog, find a nice, relaxing area and have her sit still. Start from the bottom of the paw up, pushing the fur up from the toes with your hand and with the brush. Let a little hair drop down and brush in the direction the hair grows, then use your comb to go through the hair to ensure you haven't brushed past any mats. Don't cut mats out with scissors, as you could cut the dog's skin in the process.

The brush and comb you choose should last for the life of the dog, so buy the highest-quality products you can afford. Your primary consideration should be the dog's coat type. *Natural-bristle brushes*, suited to short-haired dogs like Greyhounds and Pugs, are best because they best distribute natural oil throughout the hair and lift away dust and dirt. They are also good for finishing off the long hair of Afghans, Setters, and Spaniels, but they won't get through tangles. *Nylon brushes* offer similar results and give added lift to a long coat. *Pin brushes* have pins instead of bristles and are designed to move through a long coat and separate the

CARING FOR YOUR BRUSHES

To clean your brush, sweep a metal comb through it to remove any dead hair, then wipe the bristles with a damp facecloth. If the dog was extremely dirty or dusty, tap the brush down on a hard surface to loosen any debris. Don't submerge your brushes in water, because that will likely loosen the bristles or pins.

hairs so there's less opportunity for the hair to mat. When selecting a pin brush, run your hand over it to see how it feels. The better ones will have rounded edges on the pins so they won't hurt the dog's skin. Finally, a *slicker brush* has stainless steel teeth to move through the coat and remove the loose dead hair.

An *undercoat rake* looks like a small handheld rake. It is used to remove tangles from the undercoat of a dog with a double coat, like a Samoyed or a Collie or Keeshond, without destroying the coat.

Mat splitters are designed to cut through mats in the hair and must be used carefully since there is a blade involved. Better to prevent matting by grooming regularly than to have to go through the painstakingly slow process of mat removal.

Combs

A comb should flow through the dog's hair without catching it. Some have wider teeth at one end and more closely spaced teeth at the other end, which allows you to use it on different types of coats (the wider spaces would be better for a Poodle's coat, for example). Antistatic combs are available. Some combs have an extra row of teeth to help remove the dog's undercoat.

Specialized combs include *flea combs*, some made with Teflon to allow them to move more smoothly through the dog's coat. Flea combs have tiny,

LONG COATS NEED CARE

If you have a puppy with a long coat and want to keep her coat long, start working with a professional groomer early on to ensure that the coat will be properly cared for as it grows. The coat texture will change when the dog is between the ages of nine and fifteen months, and the result can be a matted mess if it's not properly cared for during this transitional phase.

closely spaced teeth to help catch fleas and their eggs and remove them from the dog's coat. *Untangler combs* have rotating teeth to help remove tangles, though regular grooming should help eliminate that problem.

If your dog has a very smooth coat, like a Miniature Pinscher or Greyhound, use a chamois mitt, sisal grooming glove, or horsehair glove to remove loose hair and make the coat shine. Wire mitts effectively remove excess hair, making them ideal for finishing the grooming of dogs with rough coats.

Shampoo and Conditioner

There are countless shampoos and conditioners on the market, each claiming to do something special for your dog's skin and coat. Some are supposedly formulated to enhance coat color, others to enhance texture, others to make the coat shine.

If your dog has a dark coat that tends to show flakes, you can minimize this effect by using a conditioning shampoo, an oatmeal shampoo, or a shampoo formulated especially for dry skin. Choose a shampoo formulated especially for dogs, *not* one that's formulated for people. A hypoallergenic shampoo is always a good choice.

Specialized shampoos are available to treat skin conditions and parasite infestations. Flea and tick shampoos are an important part of your flea and tick prevention program; ask your veterinarian which product is best for your dog. If your dog develops skin problems, your veterinarian can recommend a shampoo formulated for your dog's specific condition.

Tricks of the Trade

Be careful to remove all traces of shampoo by rinsing thoroughly using warm water—then, when you think the dog has been rinsed thoroughly, rinse her again. The hair will actually squeak when it's clean—yes, it truly will be squeaky clean.

Deodorizers

Another must-have for your new dog home is an odor neutralizer to help clean up accidents from carpet, upholstery, and bedding. The best of these products contain enzymes that neutralize the smell so your dog won't urinate or defecate again in the same spot. Dogs' sense of smell is far more acute than that of humans, so remember that just because you can't smell a mess after wiping it up doesn't mean that your dog can't. Simple room sprays might please your nose and help you to forget the aroma, but you should use something that will help your dog forget it as well.

Toys

Have a toy or two waiting for your new dog before she comes home for the first time—what a nice way to welcome her to the family! Like children, dogs have a way of amassing a collection of toys; and just as with children's toys, dogs' toys should be purchased with safety in mind. Because there's no regulatory agency governing pet toy safety, it's the owner's responsibility to buy the safest toys possible. This will require some thought and common sense. For soft toys, examine the toys carefully for any seams that might pull open. If you're choosing a squeaky toy, check to see that the squeaker can't be easily removed by an industrious dog. Avoid toys that your dog could swallow whole.

A wide array of dog toys are available, including soft cuddly ones that can be chewed. If you're getting your dog from a breeder, ask the breeder to rub her own scent on the soft toy and put it with the puppy's mother and littermates so the newcomer will have something with a familiar scent when she moves into her new home. Another soft toy is especially created for orphans but can bridge the gap for a puppy moving into a new home and sleeping alone for the first time. Shaped like a puppy, it has a compartment inside to hold a battery that operates a simulated heartbeat, and a pack that can be warmed in the microwave and slipped inside. The puppy can't remove either, but can cuddle up to something soft and warm with a "heartbeat."

Tricks of the Trade

Dogs love to chew, but those dental toys must be safe and not so hard that the puppy or dog will break a tooth.

Some toys have a hollow opening where you can place biscuits, a bit of peanut butter, or doggy toothpaste to keep the dog occupied. These make a nice treat to give to the puppy or dog if you have to leave her for short periods as it will keep her busy and lessen the chance of her developing separation anxiety. Another toy that keeps the puppy busy and engages her mind is a cube toy that has a sort of maze that holds kibble inside. The dog has to knock the cube around until pieces of kibble work their way out. Another toy holds biscuits, and she must figure out how to release them.

When it comes to balls and some of the hollow toys, be certain that they cannot get caught inside the dog's throat. Accidents like that have happened. It's best if you supervise your dog while she's playing with a new toy.

Tug toys (those that have a rope on one end and are held on one end by a human and held by the dog at the other end) are not always appropriate. Unless the owner knows how to control the game properly, it can get out of hand. The dog learns to be mouthy and aggressive and to take things away from the owner. This is a hot-button topic among trainers— but those who approve of the game forget that while they are experienced and know how to control it, the average pet owner often is not. There's an added hazard, especially for toy dogs: dogs can be injured if swung around at the end of a tug toy, and they can have their teeth pulled out of alignment while playing in this manner. It's important to note this rule of thumb: no play, except for a canine athlete chasing a Frisbee, should lift the dog off the ground. And no human should do this.

Tricks of the Trade

Playing with your dog is a great way to incorporate exercise, a stimulating environment, and a chance for bonding. But when outdoors beware of wet sticks. They break easily and can become lodged in your dog's throat. Splinters or pieces of wood can work their way through the dog's body and become lodged within the dog, requiring surgery.

Books and Videos

You'll want to add some reading material to your home in preparation for the newcomer. If you're buying training books and videos, find those that promote the gentlest methods. The newest training methods include clickers (those little cricket-like toys that "mark" the dog's correct response with a consistent auditory cue).

If you're acquiring a purebred you need at least one breed book. If you're adopting a mixed-breed dog, there are books dedicated to that topic as well.

Tricks of the Trade

Clicker training is a positive, powerful, gentle training method that allows the dog and human to work in perfect harmony while having fun. The end result is a wonderfully well-trained dog who responds happily—a true win–win situation.

You can also find books and videos that will show you how to groom your dog.

Other Items to Consider

Any visit to a pet supply store will prove that many products and accessories are available that can enhance your care of and relationship with your dog.

Grooming Tables

Grooming tables are a good purchase if you plan to do most or all of your dog's grooming yourself. A grooming table is a simple, stand-alone table with a nonskid rubber mat built into it. A grooming arm can be purchased separately: it can be attached to the table and holds the dog's leash or a grooming noose while the dog is standing on the table. Be aware that this can give you a false sense of security, as even the most well-trained dog left alone can become distracted and jump off the table, hanging herself by the noose.

The table will fold up for easy storage and should be purchased with safety in mind. It should be sturdy, with leg caps that don't fall off. The mat itself should be securely attached to the table and should be of a durable nonskid rubber.

Exercise Pens

Exercise pens, or *x-pens*, as they're often called, are portable gates that create a safe play area for your dog when traveling, at a dog show, or in your own home. A puppy playpen version also has a portable floor and a top to enclose puppies so they can't scramble out and get into mischief.

Clippers and Scissors

Clippers and scissors come in a wide range of sizes, styles, and prices. What you need and how much you spend will depend on the type of grooming you plan to do. If you're serious about show presentation and plan to do the dog's grooming yourself, you'll invest in more expensive equipment. If you simply want to keep your pet neat but don't want the expense of having your dog professionally groomed, you'll choose something less expensive. A groomer, pet supply store, or your veterinarian can help you decide which would be best for your dog's type of coat.

Tricks of the Trade

If you're new to grooming, remember to be very careful. Dogs can get painful nicks or razor burns while being groomed. Don't rush it!

Carriers

Little dogs are often toted everywhere—even on airplanes, where they can board with you as long as they're in a safe carry bag that will fit under the seat. A variety of companies manufacture these bags. Some are of lighter weight than others. Be certain that the one you choose is safe enough to fit under the seat but not collapse on the dog. It should be well ventilated and comfortable.

Some bags come with wheels, others with an area underneath into which you can slip an ice pack or a warming pad, depending on the weather. Some come with a separate pouch in which you can carry something extra, like an emergency can of dog food in case there are flight delays.

Car Seats

Dogs can travel safely in their crates, but some people choose to put their little dogs into a car seat instead. (Some dogs prefer to be able to see out the window.) These come in a range of styles, from a basic seat to a wide, thick seat that's well padded. A connecting strap allows you to connect the seat belt to the dog's harness. One manufacturer's car seat has a pull-out tray under the seat to hold a dish, toy, food, or treats. A lookout seat is available for dogs who want to see out the window.

Sweaters, T-Shirts, and Coats

Canine clothing has practical applications and is more than just a novelty. Small dogs lose heat more rapidly than larger dogs. And shorthaired dogs will appreciate a warm sweater or coat in the winter or a T-shirt on a cool summer day.

Backpacks and boots are useful if you plan to hike with your dog, as are folding water dishes. The assortment of items available for your new dog is seemingly endless.

Seat Belts

There are seat belts designed for dogs, but they must fit properly or they might cause more harm than good. The seat belt attaches to the car's seat belt or cargo hooks in SUVs, vans, or trucks.

What We've Learned

Chamois mitt: Placed over the owner's hand, this grooming device is best for dogs with smooth coats

Guillotine: A type of nail trimmer that has an elongated area into which the dog's nail is placed and squeezed off

Lead: Another term for a leash

Martingale collar: A collar that has one thick side and tightens on the other to prevent the dog from slipping the collar

Mat splitter: A grooming device that contains a blade, which cuts through mats in the hair

Slicker brush: A brush that has stainless steel teeth to move through the dog's coat and remove loose, dead hair

Undercoat rake: Used to remove tangles from the undercoat of a dog

Untangler comb: Has rotating teeth to help remove tangles

5

Nutritionally Sound

Veterinarians and pet owners have
come to appreciate the importance
of nutrition in the long-term health
of dogs and the prevention and
management of diseases.
— *Rebecca L. Remillard, Ph.D., D.V.M.,*
Diplomate, A.C.V.N.

Just like their owners, dogs need to eat a balanced diet in order to help maintain their physical health. There is no one best diet for every dog—you and your veterinarian should decide which diet works for your dog, taking multiple factors into consideration, including his size and activity level.

All dogs should be fed a nutritionally balanced, age-appropriate diet. Owners should use feeding methods that promote moderate growth rates and minimize obesity, musculoskeletal diseases, and behavioral problems such as finicky eating or begging.

What Should I Feed?

Every dog's diet should be formulated to meet the standards set forth by the Association of American Feed Control Officials (AAFCO). Look for the AAFCO statement on the label of your dog's food.

Tricks of the Trade

There is no need to supplement any of the diets from a reputable pet food company—they have been formulated to meet the dog's nutritional needs.

Pet food labels can be a resource in helping you decide which food is right for your dog. They contain information about some of the nutrients contained in the food. Ingredients are listed by wet weight, with the heaviest ingredient listed first. Keep in mind that if several variations of corn

PRESERVATIVES

Though the use of preservatives in pet foods is somewhat controversial, they do play a vital role in keeping food fresh and extending its shelf life. The legal maximum allowed in pet foods was recently lowered by the FDA, which gave rise to speculation that it might be unsafe. However, most food products already contained far less than the new lower maximum allowed. The pet press paid a good deal of attention to this problem, which, in turn, raised awareness that pet owners are leery of artificial preservatives. So pet food manufacturers began to use mixed tocopherols (lipid-soluble antioxidants) as preservatives. While these are natural, they don't have the long-lasting effect of the artificial preservatives, so the shelf life of pet foods with them is much shorter.

(for example) are listed, if added together those might combine to make corn the largest-percentage ingredient in the food. A complete and balanced dog food will include feeding guidelines on the label and will indicate how the food was determined to be complete and balanced.

The information on the label has to meet state requirements modeled on AAFCO guidelines, as well as criteria established by the Food and Drug Administration (FDA) and the United States Department of Agriculture (USDA). The Pet Food Institute (PFI) Nutrition Assurance Program also has some input in the information found on the label.

Talk with your veterinarian about which is better for your dog: a dry food or a canned (wet) food. Dry food such as kibble must be chewed, which is good for his teeth; however, canned food contains more water and fat, which may be more appropriate for your dog.

More than one owner has opened can after can of food hoping for a flavor the dog would like, or added filet mignon or prime rib to the food

FOOD HYPERSENSITIVITY

Sometimes a dog becomes allergic to something he is eating—not necessarily to commercial pet food, but to an ingredient in the pet food. He may have an allergic reaction to chicken or beef, for example. In order to determine the allergy, the dog is put on a restricted diet that does not contain any of the previously fed ingredients. (You should consult with your veterinarian about diet selection.) This is how the lamb and rice diet was first used: lamb and rice is not hypoallergenic per se, it simply was not commonly used in pet food, so it could be used to help determine an allergy. Today it's a popular pet food formula, so the canine allergist must use something that is not commonly fed to dogs in order to create a diet to test for allergies.

Occasionally a dog is allergic to his feeding dish, which is an example of contact hypersensitivity. In this case, replacing the dish solves the problem because the dog is no longer in contact with the irritant.

to entice the dog into eating. The result is often a dog who picks at his food and doesn't eat a balanced diet. If you find yourself begging him to eat while he tries to manipulate you into giving him something else, you are already well on the road to making food too important and creating a very spoiled, fussy eater. Keep a calm demeanor and don't fuss over the dog when he's eating.

If your dog's coat is shiny, his eyes are bright, and he's healthy and in good condition, the food you're feeding him is fine. If, on the other hand, his coat is dull and his eyes aren't sparkling, and his body condition isn't good, then it's time to think about changing to another food from a reputable company.

FEEDING YOUR PUPPY RIGHT FROM THE START

Good feeding habits will help your puppy grow into a healthy, well-behaved dog. Start early, preferably as soon as you bring your puppy home, and establish a pattern for mealtimes according to the following guidelines:

- Use a pet food specifically designed for puppies until about one year of age.
- Feed your puppy individually four times a day until he is eight to twelve weeks old, then three times a day until six months of age, then two times a day until he's one year old. Adult dogs can be fed once or twice a day, depending on owner convenience and the feeding pattern that the dog prefers. Adult toy dogs and large or Giant breeds usually do better on two meals per day.
- At each meal, offer a measured amount of food for fifteen minutes. After this time, remove all food and do not offer any other foods until the next meal.
- Treats, snacks, and table foods are not recommended. Giving your dog these foods can create an obese, begging, finicky pet. Treats should be saved for training and rewarding and should be figured into the dog's total caloric daily intake. You may also choose to use some of your dog's kibble to train.

First, seek veterinary advice. You can try another product from the same company, or give another company's product a shot. Just be sure to change the food gradually, over a four-day period, or you may cause digestive upsets. Add the new food in quarter-portions to each meal each day while removing the same amount of the old food until the changeover is complete.

Don't dismiss some of the older, more established types of food. Just because a company has created newer, more expensive products doesn't mean that there's anything wrong with their older product. If it's working for your dog, if he's eating it and is in good condition, the product is fine.

How Much Should I Feed?

The amount of food your dog should eat is based on his weight and activity level. Your food label will recommend a *daily* amount that is appropriate for your dog's weight range—don't forget to divide that amount into the number of meals that he eats each day. For example, if your dog weighs twenty pounds and the bag says that he should eat one cup of food per day, give him half a cup in the morning and half a cup in the evening. The feeding guidelines on the package are only starting points; feel free to adjust the amount you feed according to your dog's response to the amount of food.

Very small dogs (twenty pounds and under) will do better if their food is divided into two or more meals per day, usually breakfast and dinner. And very large dogs and deep-chested dogs may also do better on more than one meal per day, as they are the ones most likely to suffer from *gastric dilatation-volvulus* (GDV), a rapid-onset, often fatal condition in which air accumulates in the stomach and ultimately causes it to rotate. Dividing the dog's daily ration of food is thought to lower the risk of this condition.

Dividing meals also allows dogs to maintain their bodies' needs more efficiently over the course of the day. Yet another benefit of feeding two meals per day is that the dog eats breakfast and dinner when the family eats, which can minimize begging.

When Should I Feed?

Feeding your dog at a regular time is best for several reasons:

- Dogs appreciate routine.
- Scheduled eating will prevent your dog from becoming picky and help him maintain a proper weight.
- If your dog loses his appetite for any reason, you'll be aware of it sooner if he's on a regular schedule than you would if you were free feeding. The sooner you notice appetite changes, the sooner you can get your dog to the veterinarian if necessary.

Food should be put down for no more than fifteen minutes. If your dog doesn't finish his meal within that amount of time, pick it up and wait for the next scheduled mealtime. The only exception to this rule is a very small dog or puppy who may be predisposed to hypoglycemia (low blood sugar). This often happens with very young puppies who leave their mother too soon, and with Toy breeds such as the Maltese. It's a good idea to keep some corn syrup on hand just in case you need it to revive the puppy, or you can use a mixture of sugar and water: simply put some of the syrup or sugar water on the puppy's gums and he should revive fairly quickly. If an attack of hypoglycemia is not immediately treated, death is the likely outcome, so supervise your dog closely if he is hypoglycemic.

Where Should I Feed?

The placement of your dog's food dish is a matter of personal preference. It can be advantageous to feed him in the kitchen, where the family often eats. Usually kitchen floors are easily cleaned, so spills from your dog's food and water should not be a problem. Another option is to put a place-mat under your dog's dishes to keep the area clean.

Special Needs and Specialized Diets

Though most foods on the market are fine for most dogs, it's not unusual for a dog to need a more specialized diet to address his particular nutritional and health needs.

Recent research has shown that large- and Giant-breed puppies should eat a diet designed to allow them to grow slowly so their bones and joints will develop properly. Diets especially formulated to meet the special needs of large-breed puppies are now commercially available.

The athletic or very active dog will do best on a high-calorie, easily digested diet. Feed him four hours before exercise or within two hours after exercise. He may be fed small amounts while he's exercising. Water is, of course, the most essential nutrient, and it's especially important for the active dog's high metabolism. Diarrhea, which is common in working dogs, causes dogs to lose electrolytes.

Veterinary Diets

Veterinary, or therapeutic, diets are formulated to meet the needs of dogs with health issues (for example, cardiac problems or diabetes). Your veterinarian will tell you when one is necessary and which formula is needed. Several major pet food manufacturers now make veterinary diets. You should be able to find one that your dog will find palatable. Sometimes warming the canned version (emptied into a microwave-safe container) for a few seconds in the microwave will be enough to release the flavor and aroma and make it more appealing. The best food in the world can't do any good if the dog refuses to eat it.

Home Cooking

A home-cooked diet should be supervised by a veterinarian. This type of diet, which requires a good deal of work in preparation, must be supplemented in order for your dog to get the proper balance of nutrients.

Raw Food

A number of people are feeding their dogs raw meat and bones. Some add raw meat to their dog's commercial diet and, like those who feed a completely raw diet, claim that the dog's coat looks better. However, no independent studies have substantiated the claims of this diet's benefits. The raw food diet may not be balanced and poses health risks to dogs.

Nutraceuticals

Nutraceuticals are food compounds that are not nutrients but may have positive health benefits. Some owners give nutraceuticals to their dogs as

RAW FOOD IS RISKY

A bone or bone fragment in the meat can lodge itself in the dog's esophagus or puncture the intestines, either of which could result in death. And raw meat may contain potentially deadly salmonella and *E. coli*. In fact, raw meat contains many potential pathogens. Parasitic infection is one additional risk factor, and it has been documented in dogs fed raw beef.

It should be noted that the risk isn't just to the dog. An owner with a compromised immune system can contract diseases if the raw meat is not handled properly. Those who insist on using a raw diet—and some people have used it therapeutically—should at least use it under the supervision of a veterinarian.

It may be true that bones help clean teeth, but it is also true that some commercial pet foods now contain ingredients that help remove the tartar from teeth and imitate the cleaning action of chewing a bone without the risk of splintering. (These products should have the seal of acceptance of the Veterinary Oral Health Council on the package.)

dietary supplements. Glucosamine and chondroitin sulfate are probably the best-known nutraceuticals, believed to alleviate joint pain naturally (in both dogs and humans). Manufacturers do not consider these compounds drugs, because if they were labeled as such they would be subject to Food and Drug Administration (FDA) safety and efficacy testing. Companies that manufacture and sell nutraceuticals can voluntarily have their products go through an approval process to ensure that the ingredients have been manufactured to a given standard. The product must have *reproducible effects*—in other words, the manufacturer must prove that the product will always cause the same thing to happen to the individual who consumes it (for example, pain will be alleviated).

Unfortunately, it's difficult for the consumer to know which products have been proven to perform well. Nutraceuticals are subject to regulation by federal and state agencies (not in all states), but regulation is not uniformly reliable. You could buy a product, take it home, and use it in good faith without knowing that the active ingredient either is not in the product or is present in too small a quantity to be effective. In other words, you may not be getting what you're paying for. The best you can do is read the literature that comes with the product to try to ascertain whether the product has been evaluated by a university or an independent authority.

Nutraceuticals are usually available in health food stores or pharmacies. Some commercial foods now have nutraceuticals added. These cannot, however, be advertised as having any impact on health. An ad might state, for example, that "Product X contains Compound Y," and consumers might assume Compound Y is good for something.

Tricks of the Trade

Just like people, dogs need clean, fresh water. Be sure that your dog's bowl is refreshed several times a day.

Obesity

Obesity is one of the major health problems in dogs today. It has been reported that half to three-quarters of all pets seen by veterinarians are overweight or obese. Obesity in dogs, just as in humans, can lead to a variety of orthopedic, dermatological, and respiratory health problems.

Ensuring that your dog maintains a healthy weight is one of your responsibilities as a pet owner. If your dog begins to gain weight—and some breeds are predisposed to weight problems, such as Labrador Retrievers and Miniature Pinschers—you'll need to begin a weight reduction program under the guidance of your veterinarian. Recommended

ON THE LABEL

There has been some controversy about terms used on pet food labels because many people don't understand what the terms mean and therefore jump to conclusions. Here are some of the terms that have been misunderstood, along with their accurate definitions. The complete list of terms and AAFCO definitions is available in the AAFCO manual, which can be purchased from their website, aafco.org.

Balanced: A term that may be applied to a diet, ration, or feed having all known required nutrients in proper amount and proportion based on recommendations of recognized authorities in the field of animal nutrition, such as the National Research Council, for a given set of physiological animal requirements. The species for which it is intended and the functions, such as maintenance or maintenance plus production (growth, fetus, fat, milk, eggs, wool feather, or work), shall be specified.

Digests: Liquefied or powdered fats and animal tissues that are sprayed onto dry foods to enhance palatability.

Meat by-products: The nonrendered clean parts derived from slaughtered mammals, other than meat. By-products include, but are not limited to, lungs, weight loss measures might include a reduction in the amount you're currently feeding, or a special low-calorie veterinary diet. Almost certainly, exercise will be recommended. Food and water are only part of the equation—a daily walk should be the minimum amount of exercise your puppy or dog receives. Your veterinarian will want to see your dog periodically to evaluate his progress and adjust the diet as necessary.

One simple way to help your dog avoid weight problems is to limit his consumption of commercial treats, which are usually high in fat. If you're using food rewards for training purposes, remember that the reward doesn't have to be big. A tiny piece of cheese, turkey, or chicken is all that's needed—it's the message conveyed that is important. Raw, washed vegetables are a

spleen, kidneys, brain, livers, blood, bone, partially defatted low-temperature fatty tissue, and stomachs and intestines freed of their contents. They do not include hair, horns, teeth, and hooves. They shall be suitable for use in animal food.

Poultry by-product meal: Consists of the ground, rendered, clean parts of the carcass of slaughtered poultry, such as necks, feet, undeveloped eggs, and intestines, exclusive of feathers, except in such amounts as might occur unavoidably in good processing practices.

Poultry by-products: Nonrendered clean parts of carcasses of slaughtered poultry, other than meat, such as heads, feet, viscera, free from fecal content and foreign matter, except in such trace amounts as might occur unavoidably in good factory practice.

good snack for your dog. In fact, carrots make a great, healthy snack and have the added benefit of letting him chew.

Tricks of the Trade

These tests can help you determine whether your dog is overweight:

- You should be able to feel your dog's ribs.
- When you stand over him and look down, you should see a curve in his body where his "waist" would be.

Your veterinarian can show you how to do a rib check of your dog so that you will learn to feel what is right and know when your dog is gaining or losing weight.

You may be tempted to share your own snacks with him, but it's not necessary. Instead of sharing fattening snacks, share yourself with your dog: play fetch, practice a dog sport, go for a walk. There are many things you can do together other than eat. Your dog is interested in your companionship.

When dogs seek attention, the owner will often toss him a biscuit or give him more food. If you have determined that he is eating the correct amount of food for his age and weight and he's in good condition, then food is not what he's craving. Your dog is seeking more attention from you. Spend some extra time playing with him, or take him for a walk. He's eating that extra food because he's bored, and if he keeps it up he'll become overweight. Alleviate that boredom with interaction; dogs need to spend time with their family members.

Things to Avoid

Many people think the word *natural* means "wholesome" and "healthy," but that's not necessarily so. Some have been led to believe that adding "natural" supplements might help the dog's diet, but complete and balanced diets are exactly that: they don't require supplementation. While not many foods are poisonous, some "natural" foods and products can endanger your dog's health. For example, oversupplementing your dog's diet with cod liver oil could result in vitamin D toxicity, while feeding him too much liver can result in oversupplementation of vitamin A.

Theobromine, which is found in chocolate and cocoa, is hazardous to dogs. In fact, it can be fatal if ingested in a large enough amount. It is therefore best to keep chocolate products away from your pets at all times.

If a dog consumes enough onion, it can result in hemolytic anemia, which is when red blood cells rupture so that the total number of red blood cells actually decreases. Even though they can recover, some dogs have died as a result of ingesting onion.

Tricks of the Trade

Be sure to check freshness dates on any pet food that you purchase. Pet food, just like people food, can become rancid.

What We've Learned

Anemia: A low red blood cell count
Gastric dilatation-volvulus (GDV): A condition in which air accumulates in the stomach and ultimately causes the stomach to rotate
Hypoglycemia: Low blood sugar
Nutraceuticals: Over-the-counter food compounds that are not nutrients but may have positive health benefits. Used to supplement diets.
Pathogens: Disease-producing agents or microorganisms

6

Training the Right Way

The value you place on your dog is reflected in the
quality of your relationship with her. This relationship
begins the second you choose the dog and is defined
by your ability to be the guardian and human partner
she deserves. The dog your pup will become is greatly
influenced by how you teach her to behave when
she is at her youngest and neediest. Dogs raised in a
humane, stimulating, understanding, and loving
environment that meets their needs are as happy
and mentally healthy as possible.
—*Karen Overall, M.A., V.M.D., Ph.D.,*
Diplomate, A.C.V.B., ABS Certified
Applied Animal Behaviorist

The time you put into training your dog will pay dividends for her
entire life. She will be well mannered in all circumstances of
everyday life, a happy and well-adjusted member of your family,
and a welcome addition to your neighborhood. It's important to train your
dog right from the start. The bonus is that training will help build the

bond of trust between you. Your dog's behavior will be shaped by her training as much as her early life experiences and genes. It's both nature and nurture that shape a dog.

Tricks of the Trade

The veterinary community is becoming more aware of behavior issues. Recent research has shown that behavior problems are often the reason why dogs are euthanized or abandoned. If your dog has come from lines with no known behavioral problems, you have a head start. But knowing how to properly raise and train a dog is the key to your relationship—and an important part of your wellness program. Averting problems before they arise will prevent a needless death. What you expect from your dog and how well you are matched in terms of personality and lifestyle will play a part in this.

Your veterinarian will very likely question you about your dog's behavior as well as her physical condition. A routine behavior profile of your canine companion will allow your veterinarian to know if there is a problem now or one in the making. Some veterinarians might have a questionnaire that you would be asked to fill out, just as you would fill out a form pertaining to your own health at the doctor's office. (If your veterinarian doesn't have a questionnaire, there are many published ones that they can use. This is a fairly new field and not everyone will have a questionnaire at this point.) Your veterinarian will review the behavior questionnaire with you.

If your veterinarian has a special interest in behavior, she or he can provide a consultation with you, for a fee, to help with any behavior problems. Otherwise, your veterinarian can refer you to a behaviorist. There are specialists in veterinary medicine who are board certified by the American College of Veterinary Behaviorists; there are people with advanced degrees who are certified as Applied Animal Behaviorists by the Animal Behavior Society; and there's the Association of Pet Dog Trainers, who are certified trainers. Just be sure your dog's trainer uses the newest, most positive methods. Call and ask them about the methods they use. And ask if you can sit in on a session or a class.

Some owners have unrealistic expectations because they do not understand that some canine behaviors such as chewing are perfectly normal, so they have unrealistic expectations about how the dog should act. Dogs chew—it's what they do by nature. And, like children, their gums are uncomfortable when they're teething. They don't know what's acceptable in human terms, so they will chew whatever is available, especially if acceptable items like chewtoys are not available. It's to be expected that a puppy will destroy something expensive when teething, such as the rung of a chair, a pair of shoes, or a silk tie. If you're prepared for that, you will be less likely to become angry with the puppy, who really doesn't understand that she has done something wrong. It's important to provide appropriate chew toys.

Tricks of the Trade

If your dog is chewing the woodwork, or trying to chew through the wood of a window frame, she has a behavior problem. It is very likely associated with separation anxiety, as the areas she's choosing are near places where one can leave the house. Chewing furniture is another clue to a separation anxiety problem. A dog who is anxious will try to calm herself by chewing. Your pet needs to be assured that when you leave, you will always return. You can desensitize her to your coming and going by leaving for a moment and then returning, gradually increasing the time away from her in one-minute increments. Don't make a fuss when you return, or you will create more anxiety.

Separation Anxiety

A dog with separation anxiety may destroy doors, window frames, base-boards, furniture, pillows—anything is fair game because the anxious dog is stressed over her owner's absence. There may also be inappropriate elimination; this might be a sign of a physical problem, so a quick trip to your veterinarian for a checkup is in order before you label it a behavior problem.

Separation anxiety may also include a lot of barking, whining, or howl-ing. (Dogs will also bark when the owner is home in a bid for attention.) A cautious approach is desirable here. When the owner tells the dog to be quiet, the dog responds to this as something positive—she has received her owner's attention and has learned that barking gets the desired result. However, if the barking is associated with anxiety, the owner has just trained the dog to bark anxiously, which is the exact opposite of what the owner wanted. It's important to remember that barking is the dog's nor-mal means of communication. It is up to the owner to teach the dog when barking is and isn't acceptable and to not accidentally reinforce anxious behavior. Some of the nicest owners have the worst-behaved dogs because they've inadvertently reinforced bad behavior.

While you want your dog to bond with you, you do not want that bond to become distorted and produce a dog who is so anxious when left alone that she becomes neurotic. Owners can accidentally aggravate a dog's stress by rewarding what they thought was normal behavior. This can be

PET-PROOFING

A teething puppy will chew whatever is handy—including electrical cords. It's imperative that the house be *pet-proofed*, which consists of taping cords to walls and covering electrical sockets so they're less attractive objects for chewing or licking (which could lead to electrical shocks and/or burns).

avoided by training your dog to be calm and to understand that you are going to be reliable from the beginning.

Resource Guarding

Resource guarding—in other words, a dog's "protecting" her property from her humans and not allowing them to touch it—can become a serious problem. You should prevent this right from the start by teaching her to share. One of the easiest ways to do this is to teach her to "trade" you for something. When she is playing with a toy, approach her with a different toy, or one she hasn't seen in a while, then say, "Trade you!" and have your hand out under the toy she's holding. When she drops the toy she'd been playing with in order to take the new one, you take the old one and tell her, "Good girl!" A few repetitions of this should have her happily trading things. Be careful that this is an exchange and that she's not being bribed to give you whatever she's holding—there is a difference, which is made quite clear through your actions and your tone of voice. It's not wheedling, like some parents do with children. Trading will also come in handy if she has picked up something she shouldn't have, whether it's something that could endanger her or just a family member's sock or shoe. Another thing you can do to encourage her trust in you is to add a few pieces of food to her dish while she's eating. Some dogs can become resource guarders with food as the resource they don't want anyone near. This will reassure the dog that when you are near her food dish, good things happen.

Socialization

No puppy should leave its mother and littermates before twelve weeks of age unless there are extenuating circumstances, such as the mother having died. It has been discovered that puppies need that time with their mother and littermates to learn everything that they will need to know as adults, including that all-important bite inhibition, which humans cannot truly teach a dog. Bite inhibition means that the dog learns not to bite down hard on anyone. One way littermates and the mother let the puppy know when she's biting down too hard is by yelping. This teaches her that she has caused pain, so she learns not to bite down so hard the next time. Puppies use their mouths in play and don't understand, unless taught, that they should not cause pain. If they don't learn to inhibit their biting in this manner, they can cause pain or damage as adults when they have stronger teeth and jaws.

During those first twelve weeks, the breeder must facilitate the proper socialization; if a puppy isn't socialized during this time, she will likely have problems relating to people and assorted life situations. Everything should seem normal to the puppy so she accepts whatever life brings her way. During this time the breeder must also be willing to housetrain the dog. Eight and a half weeks of age is the perfect time for the puppy to learn to eliminate where it's acceptable and not eliminate where it's unacceptable.

The breeder will have to consider where the dog will ultimately be living; the puppy should have already been acclimated to a variety of places before she arrives in her new home. By the time a puppy reaches twelve weeks of age she should have experienced, on a continuing basis, a wide variety of people, places, sounds, sights, and aromas. She should also have been in the company of other species.

The total time for socialization is quite brief, and there are very severe consequences if the pups aren't socialized or if they receive very little socialization. By twelve weeks puppies enter the juvenile stage, and it is at this stage that a negative experience can desocialize the pup, so it's important to provide the most positive environment for her and ensure that all her experiences are positive ones. Unsocialized dogs won't relate well to people or other animals and they won't do well if they're left for boarding, and behavior problems are likely to occur throughout the dog's life.

The puppy should know the feel of gentle hands from her first day of life. She should have experienced being in different rooms of a house, walking on different surfaces, and meeting a variety of people.

After at least one vaccination, she should have been taken places where she would not be at great risk for disease but where she would see a wide variety of things. Making her entire world seem a very normal place is the goal. Loud noises shouldn't be unduly surprising. Trucks, cars, trains, and planes shouldn't startle a well-adjusted dog—they should simply be accepted as a part of normal life.

Taking your dog places throughout her lifetime is important so that she continues to experience the world socially and build on her early puppy socialization lessons. She also needs to experience play with other dogs because it's through this that learning occurs and natural dog instincts are developed. A puppy that has not been properly socialized can be shy, exhibit fear, and can even become a fear biter. A dog from this sort of background will require a sensitive owner who is willing to work to rehabilitate the dog.

Introducing Dogs and Children

Children need to be properly introduced to dogs. Dogs and children should be introduced slowly, carefully, and under complete adult supervision. They should never be left alone together, especially very young children and young puppies. Children often behave unpredictably and could hurt the dog. Children must be taught to be gentle with the dog, not yell, scream, run fast, or swoop down on the dog. The child must also be taught not to look the dog right in the eyes; this is considered, by dogs, to be very aggressive behavior, and therefore can lead to the child being bitten. Small children are often at eye level with medium and large or Giant dogs, which can aggravate this problem.

When you're introducing a child and a puppy, the child should sit on the floor and allow the puppy to come over and investigate. The child should never be allowed to pick up the puppy (or adult small dog) because anything a child can pick up can be dropped. Children should not be allowed to poke or prod the dog. Let the dog sniff the child's hand, preferably the knuckles so that fingers aren't offered to the dog. The child can roll a ball or toss a toy, playing a gentle game of fetch. The child should never pull the toy away from the dog. The introduction should be a positive experience for both the dog and the child.

If you're bringing a new baby home from the hospital, spend some time getting your dog acclimated to the idea of having a baby in the house. Let her see you hold a doll, let her walk around the nursery to see and smell things. Practice walking her along with the baby carriage, and change the schedule from your regular one since you will probably have to alter it after the baby arrives. Once the baby has been born, have another family member bring home a piece of clothing or a blanket that has been near the baby and let your dog smell it so she will become accustomed to the smell of your new baby. If it's possible, take a tape recorder to the hospital and tape the sound of your baby crying. Each baby has a unique sound, and a dog's hearing is sensitive. Let her hear your baby before she sees her.

When it's time for introductions, have someone else bring your dog outdoors to meet the baby before you bring the baby into the house. Always be sure that good things happen for the dog when the baby is in the room. Give your dog lots of attention when the baby is around so you don't create a version of sibling rivalry. And never leave your dog and your baby together for any amount of time without supervision.

Housetraining

As discussed earlier, eight and a half weeks is the age when a puppy can first discriminate between where she should eliminate and where she should not, so housetraining your pup should be the first thing on your training agenda. If you're planning to housetrain your new canine companion to eliminate outdoors, you must choose a spot before you bring her home. Select a place that is convenient for you but out of the mainstream of activity. It should be a fairly secluded area where she can feel comfortable about eliminating with some privacy, without having to worry about neighborhood dogs invading her space. Even if you have a fenced yard, don't send her outside alone or she'll never learn what is expected; you'll have to go with her every time. Be certain that you have a very special treat with you whenever you take her to her special spot—a treat that she gets for eliminating at the right place and at no other time. Consistency is key to housetraining.

When you bring your dog home the first time, take her to that special spot before you bring her indoors. Encourage her by using one or two words that will teach her to eliminate on command, such as "Hurry!" or "Go potty!" As soon as she has eliminated, praise her enthusiastically and give her the special treat. Repeat this performance whenever you take her to her special spot. Whenever a puppy has been playing, she'll need to go out. She'll also have to go out after she has eaten, and after a nap or any sort of confinement.

No matter where you choose to have her eliminate, remember that you must always accompany your pet so you can praise and reward her immediately. Puppies have a short attention span, about a few seconds. And remember that you must be consistent when training or you will confuse your pup and she won't learn what is expected of her. You may want to sleep through the night, but if your puppy has to eliminate you're going to have to get out of bed and take her to that chosen place.

A helpful hint: puppies can wait to eliminate only for as many hours as they are months of age until they're a year old. A three-month-old puppy should be able to wait three hours between trips to her special place.

Tricks of the Trade

You'll know your dog is housetrained when she consistently and reliably "asks" to go out, usually by going to the door. Or you can teach her to "ring" a doorbell by having hanging bells, or a specially made doggy buzzer, placed low enough for your dog to hit with her paw. Ring it every time you take her out and she'll soon learn to ring it herself. When she no longer has accidents on your floor, you can consider her fully housetrained and begin to give her access to the entire house if you desire.

Younger puppies will need to eliminate more frequently. Remember that the puppy will always need to go out after eating, drinking, napping, and exercise or play.

Your puppy will need to be closely supervised while she's being housetrained. An older dog coming into your home will need the same training and supervision, although it should take less time to train her. The older she is, the longer she can wait between elimination trips. If she was housetrained in her last home, it shouldn't take more than a few days to train her to the proper elimination spot at her new residence. Some small dogs take longer to train; sometimes a year or more will pass before they are reliably housetrained.

If your dog has an accident in the house, do not scold her. It's up to you to watch her for signs that she has to eliminate. Scolding will only frighten her and give her a negative association with you and the housetraining process. If she has defecated, remove the evidence promptly. If you catch your pet urinating, pick her up without scaring her and move her to her special spot as quickly as possible. Praise and reward her. And be sure to clean the spot with a cleaner that breaks down enzymes—if the odor lingers in that spot, she will think that's the place to eliminate.

Puppies that come from a pet store, puppy mill or commercial breeder, or backyard breeder probably have not experienced a clean environment and will be more difficult to housetrain. If they're accustomed to being surrounded by their own waste they are less likely to be concerned about being clean. This doesn't mean that your dog can't be housetrained or won't come to prefer a clean environment. It just means that it will probably take longer to train her and you should be prepared to be patient.

Crate Training

The canine instinct to sleep in a crate probably goes back thousands of years to the dog's earlier ancestors, who would find a safe den where they could sleep, groom each other, lick their wounds, keep warm, have babies, and take care of their young while avoiding predators or humans. While many of these needs are now met differently in domestic dogs, a crate can be a safe haven where dogs can retreat and be protected from their otherwise busy world. When dogs are raised properly from the beginning, not pushed together in overcrowded conditions, and given the opportunity to remain clean, they want to continue to remain clean, which is why a crate is such a wonderful housetraining tool: they won't soil the place where they sleep.

A crate also has the advantage of being multifunctional. It can serve as your dog's car seat when traveling, or a bed, or a safe haven in the house. A crate is not meant to be used as a punishment device; you cannot leave your dog in the closed crate for endless hours and expect it to be an effective training tool or a place where she will want to be.

Buy a crate that's safe, without large openings so your dog won't be injured trying to escape through a small hole or get her license or identification tag caught. The crate should be just big enough for her to stand up and turn around in when she's full grown. Make that crate as attractive as possible by making it comfortable and putting a safe toy inside.

Before your dog is housetrained you'll want to line the crate with newspaper and then put soft, washable bedding on top. A large, fluffy towel can serve this purpose. After she's reliably housetrained, you can buy a special crate pad that will serve as a mattress. Crates often are equipped with

THE PACK

A *pack* is the name for a social and extended family group of dogs, just as *school* is the name for the same grouping in fish. Feral or homeless dogs may form true packs and meet the social, communal hunting and feeding, and extended family criteria. Humans and their dogs have much looser social affiliations with a very different social structure than in true packs, but the human–canine household social unit is often colloquially called a pack. Quiet simply, most dogs now are referred to by their people as "family," a description that has looser requirements for social grouping.

CRATE TRAINING

HOW AND WHY TO USE THIS EFFECTIVE TRAINING TOOL

The dog crate is a wonderful training tool. Apart from its obvious uses for transporting dogs by car or plane, the crate may be used for short-term confinement to keep the dog out of mischief at times when the owner is not able to supervise. Confining the dog to the crate prevents her from developing bad habits. In addition, the crate may be used specifically to create good household habits: to housetrain the dog, to establish a chew toy habit, and to reduce hyperactivity and barking. However, sometimes crate training backfires, and misuse of the crate by novice owners may produce a dog that is more difficult to housetrain, more active and unruly, more vocal and destructive, and maybe aggressive!

Misuse Equals Abuse

Crate training problems usually arise because owners fail to teach the dog to like the crate, and leave untrained dogs confined for too long. If the owner has not gotten the dog accustomed to the crate, she will not enjoy confinement, and might run from the owners when called and/or resist and resent being manhandled into the crate. Once confined, the dog might bark out of frustration and try to destroy the crate in an attempt to escape. If confined for too long, the dog will soil the crate.

Whether an adult dog likes her crate depends on when and how the crate was initially introduced. If the dog was taught to enjoy it during puppyhood, she will prefer resting in her doggy den as an adult (this is easily tested by leaving the crate door open).

However, an adolescent dog allowed complete freedom of house and garden since puppyhood might object to lengthy confinement unless previously trained to enjoy the crate.

Introducing the Crate

No matter how much the dog enjoys the crate, there will be occasions when it will be necessary to confine the dog against her wishes. Therefore, never call the dog and put her in the crate, or else she will soon become wary of approaching you when called. Instead, use a place command: "Go to your crate." It is possible to enforce a place command without ruining the dog's recall.

Tell the dog, "Go to your crate," lure her toward the crate with a food treat (kibble from dinner), and give the lure as a reward when she settles down inside. Praise the dog and periodically hand-feed kibble while she is inside, but ignore her the moment she leaves. Feed the dog in the crate. Place pieces of kibble in the crate so the dog will develop the habit of visiting the crate on her own. And whenever she does, praise her and offer especially tasty food treats, ignoring her when she leaves. The dog will soon learn she gets lots of attention, affection, and goodies inside the crate, but very little outside.

Now get the dog accustomed to short confinement. Throw a treat in the crate and close the door long enough to give her two or three tasty treats through the gate, then open the crate. Repeat this many times over. It is important that the dog learn that confinement does not necessarily mean "for the duration," but rather for a short time and a good time.

Place Training

A dog crate is a marvelous place to send the dog when the house gets busy or when the owner just wants a little peace and quiet. It is important to familiarize the dog with the crate as early on as possible so that controlled, quiet periods set the precedent for adult life. Learning to "turn the dog off"—to frequently instruct her to settle down and shush—is a priority obedience exercise for pet owners.

The length of time a dog may be confined to a crate depends on whether she enjoys the crate and whether she is housetrained. To confine an unhousetrained dog to a crate for lengthy periods is courting disaster. If the dog is forced to soil her sleeping area, the crate may no longer be effective in inhibiting elimination, and therefore cannot be used as a predicting tool in housetraining.

Housetraining

A dog crate may be used effectively as a housetraining tool. Housesoiling is a spatial problem, and confinement is the solution: the dog is eliminating in the wrong place, and if confined and not allowed free access to the living rooms and bedrooms, she cannot soil the carpets.

During housetraining, the purpose of short-term close confinement (crate training) is to inhibit the dog from eliminating at all. Then the dog will want to eliminate immediately when released from confinement and taken to her toilet area (outside).

The single most important use of the crate for housetraining is as a tool to predict when the dog will eliminate. When at home, confine her to the crate in the same room as the family, so she does not become socially isolated. Every hour, run the dog to her elimination area outside and give her three minutes to produce. If she does, praise and give food treats. If she doesn't, put her back in the crate for another hour.

From the Animal Wellness Program at Angell Memorial Animal Hospital

a detachable water dish. Be sure that the water dish is always clean and filled with fresh water.

Try not to leave your dog in a crate for an entire day while you're at work. Preferably, someone should go home at lunchtime to take the dog for a walk. If you must leave her crated, buy a large crate and separate it into two sections: one half is set off as a potty area and the other is for sleeping. If you can, arrange to leave her in a room that's set up for her comfort during the day with a potty area or access to a fenced-in, safe area of your yard. She should have fresh water available. And it would be thoughtful to leave a radio on so she can hear human voices and won't feel totally alone.

Tricks of the Trade

A crate is the best place for your dog to be while in a car. It's familiar and comforting to her and is as safe as a baby's car seat. If you've chosen a plastic crate, be sure to secure it using a seat belt.

Crate training enables you to teach your dog about the importance of and need for separation. A dog who is too dependent on her owner can develop separation anxiety. Closing your dog in the crate for a few minutes every day while you're in the room will teach her that she cannot always be glued to your side. She can see and hear you, but she has to learn to play by herself or rest for a bit. If she begins to cry, do not let her have her way. Letting her out of the crate on demand will spoil her and will reinforce her negative behavior. When she stops crying, let her rejoin you outside the crate.

Some rescue or shelter dogs have had a negative association with the crate because it has been used as punishment. While you may want to try to habituate the dog to the crate and make it a pleasant association, you cannot expect to do that and housetrain her at the same time. In this case, you can tether the dog to you. Get a long leash and tie one end of it to your belt, so that wherever you go, the dog goes. You'll know when she needs to go out because she'll be close to you, and you'll also be aware of her movements or any restlessness she may exhibit. You can also put baby gates up to give the dog a small amount of room in the house in which to roam, put a bell on her collar or harness, and listen for that bell. When the bell stops, you need to check the dog immediately because she may need to eliminate, and you need to take her to the right place.

Litterbox Training

A fairly new training method, litterbox training can be accomplished in the same way as training to eliminate outdoors. You'll need to accompany your dog to the litterbox, praise her, and give her a special reward. You can use newspaper to line the litterbox or one of the new litters designed for dogs.

Food Reward Training

Food reward training is exactly what it sounds like. Very tiny bits of a favorite food (like chicken, cheese, or minuscule bits of cooked liver) are used, along with praise, to promptly reward the dog for doing what she has been asked to do. You can also use part of her daily ration of kibble. The only thing that differs from clicker training is the lack of the clicker as an event marker. You will be relying on your voice and the treat. The goal is to happily train the dog but not unbalance her diet.

Manners and More

To facilitate the owner–dog relationship, and to further solidify your bond with your dog, it is important that you be the "leader" from whom all good things emanate. Your dog needs to learn not to jump up on people, not to bark excessively, and to behave in ways that are acceptable to humans. It's strongly recommended that you sign your dog up for obedience classes so she will learn proper manners with other dogs.

Obedience Classes

Choose an instructor who uses the most positive training methods, with no more than a simple buckle collar. Some trainers use head collars, also called a *halter*. Ensure that the trainer has been properly trained in the use of a head collar, as it has the ability to cause physical damage when used by an untrained individual. Never use one on your own. A harness can work well for small dogs with a collapsing trachea or those that are predisposed to that condition. The trainer should be using positive reinforcement, whether it's food reward training or clicker training. And be certain that puppies are sorted out by size during class play periods so that a tiny puppy isn't accidentally injured by a larger one.

Tricks of the Trade

Finding a good obedience class or puppy kindergarten will require some investigation. You can ask your veterinarian or the person from whom you got your dog if they can recommend someone. Or go to clickertraining.com and look for clicker trainers in your area. Once you've located someone in your area, ask to observe a class before enrolling. Be certain that the trainer is experienced and that he separates the puppies for play period. A three-month-old Newfoundland puppy and a three-month-old Chihuahua puppy might be the same age and enjoy playing together, but the Chihuahua could easily be injured during enthusiastic puppy play. Also watch to see that only the gentlest methods are used and that potential bullies aren't allowed to intimidate the other puppies.

Sit and Wait

One of the easiest and most effective ways to teach your dog that you are the leader and that barking, jumping up on people, and such aren't acceptable behaviors, is to make her sit and wait for all good things. She sits before her food dish is placed on the floor; she sits to be patted when people come to visit. She can't jump up if she's sitting. Jumping up is a canine greeting behavior to elicit attention. If she doesn't receive the attention she craves until she sits, she'll soon learn not to jump on people.

Clicker Training

Clicker training (operant conditioning) is a simple and positive method of dog training that produces quick results. The clicker serves as an event marker to "tell" the dog that she has done the right thing. The sound of the click is far more consistent than the human voice saying, "Good," although you should add praise too. The click tells the dog that she is doing the right thing, pinpointing exactly what she's being rewarded for doing, making it easy for her to understand exactly what you want. Learning happens much faster than with food, or praise without the click.

You click, praise, and reward with a treat. The "treat" need not be food, although that works extremely well. Some dogs prefer their reward to be a favorite toy, or a loving pat. You can find what best motivates your individual dog. And the clicker doesn't have to be a formal clicker. You can also use a barrette, ballpoint pen, or a cap from a baby-food jar—anything that makes a consistent clicking sound.

If the sound of a clicker is too loud for your dog, try one of the alternatives or hold the clicker in your pocket, or wrap it in something to muffle the sound. Dogs have very acute hearing. If there's something special that you want to teach your dog, use a different treat that the dog only gets for that particular activity. This is known as a high-value reward. Tiny bits of hot dog are often favored as a high-value reward.

If you decide to clicker train (and there are classes as well as books and videos available to teach this easy training method), remember to teach that click equals treat before starting to train the first time. Clicker training is like a game for your dog. She "wins" by discovering for herself that she can make you click. Her reward is actually the click (which is used in place of the word *good* because it is more consistent than the human voice). The treat becomes a bonus. When she does something especially well, give her several treats at once. This is called a *jackpot*.

Whatever you set out to teach must be done in slow steps. Break down each new behavior into small, separate parts. Once your dog has the basics down, then you can begin to train for specific behaviors. After a few repetitions, begin to vary the number of times she does something correctly before you click and treat so that she will improve her performance. She can, for example, show you a straighter sit. You can build a better or longer sit, or a sit in the presence of distractions, by clicking for little improvements, across several brief training sessions.

Don't teach the verbal cue until you're certain that your dog can repeat the behavior reliably—then you can add the word. She will quickly learn to associate the word with the behavior for which she is being clicked. The words are only a distraction in the beginning. The only thing your dog should hear from you is praise until she is reliably performing the task you're training. Always follow the click with the treat. When your dog knows what the word means, and always does the right thing, you can start replacing the click and treat with just a praise word and a pat. Soon you'll be able to save your click and treat for learning the next new thing!

Keep training sessions short, only a few minutes a day, and always end on a high note. Be sure that your dog does something right before you end the training session, even if you have to return to something basic. Watch for signs of stress your dog might display such as yawning, licking, or turning her head away.

Barking

All dogs bark, but excessive barking is simply unacceptable to humans. Different breeds have different barking propensities. You will not, for example, ever have a silent Beagle or Shetland Sheepdog. There are different ways to approach problem barking. One is to reward the dog only when she is quiet. Another is to put the barking on cue—in other words, you train her to bark so that you are in control of the barking. She has the release of being able to bark, but only when the owner deems it acceptable. You wouldn't want to eliminate all barking since you will very likely want your dog to tell you when, for example, a stranger is on your property.

Some dogs like to bark when they're excited about an activity—it's their way of expressing themselves. Dogs can usually be trained to be quiet during the activity, knowing that they'll receive a special treat afterward.

You can click and treat for barking. Show her the flat of your hand, using it like a traffic cop's stop signal, while the dog is eating the treat, and then click her and treat her again for silence. If you do this a few times, clicking the bark and then giving her the hand signal and clicking the silence, you will see the dog giving a calming signal—turning her head or averting her eyes—from the flat hand, and then you can click and treat for that. You will very quickly get a silence signal, which you can then use when the dog is barking for her own reasons. Be ready with the click and treat and don't expect more than a second or two of silence at first, then two or three or five seconds.

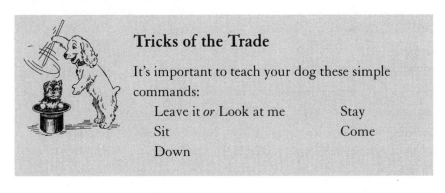

Tricks of the Trade

It's important to teach your dog these simple commands:

Leave it *or* Look at me	Stay
Sit	Come
Down	

Leave It *or* Look at Me

One of the most important things you can teach your dog is the command "Leave it!" or "Look!" or "Look at me!" A curious canine can inadvertently get into all manner of trouble—there are too many things that interest the dog but can be dangerous if swallowed. With a trained response to verbal commands, the dog will ignore what she is about to pick up.

The easiest way to train this is to click and treat for any eye movement toward you. Slowly build this up to head movement until you have her reliably looking at you when you say, "Look at me!" Or you can click her for ignoring a favorite toy. Click and treat for any movement away from that and toward something that you have. This can also be turned into "Trade!" when you have her swap the favored toy she's holding for one that you have in your hand. Each of these choices will produce a happy dog who will be responsive to her owner and less likely to swallow something she shouldn't (unless, of course, she is unsupervised). Patrolling the

PICA AND COPROPHAGIA

Pica is an abnormal desire to eat things that are indigestible. A number of dogs seem to do this. Often those dogs will choose to eat dirt, rocks, socks, sticks, whatever is handy. Some breeds may be predisposed; for example, no one knows why, but Chesapeake Bay Retrievers are often rock eaters. If your dog consumes odd items, have your veterinarian check her for any possible health problems or deficiencies. If there are none, your veterinarian is likely to assume that it's a behavior problem. Pica is generally considered to be a form of obsessive-compulsive disorder (OCD). One of the best things that you can do is keep your dog busy and active so her mind is occupied with other things. Pica begins in puppyhood but can often last into adulthood.

Puppies and some adult dogs will eat their own excrement or that of other animals. This is called *coprophagia*, and it is a form of pica. The dog may view this as acceptable because she can see her mother eating her puppies' excrement in an effort to keep the whelping box clean. Responsible breeders, however, are usually quite good about cleaning up the whelping box before the mother can so the puppies always experience a clean area. The best way to deal with coprophagia in dogs is to clean up before they have a chance to consume the excrement. While it has been suggested that hot sauce or something unpleasant tasting may be poured on the excrement to deter the dog from eating it, cleaning up rapidly and distracting the dog are probably more effective techniques. Call the dog away from the excrement and ask her to sit and give her a very tasty reward, something that will be more appealing to her than the excrement.

house and yard for small items that are likely to be swallowed, such as pins, paper clips, and such, will still be a necessary safeguard.

Sit

Teaching a dog to sit is very easy. Clicker trainers simply wait for the dog to sit, then they click and treat. A few repetitions is all it takes for the dog to learn that she can make you click by sitting; dogs understand clicker training a lot faster than people do!

If you're less patient and want immediate results you can lure the dog into a sitting position. It's easy to do. Take a treat in one hand and move that hand from in front of the dog, up, and over her head a couple of inches until your hand is between her ears. She'll have to sit while she looks up. Click and treat as soon as her rear end touches the floor. Or praise and treat if you're not clicker training. Remember to use a lure only a couple of times. You have to fade it after a few repetitions. Don't lure her into a sitting position too many times or your dog will come to focus only on the presence of the food instead of on what she is supposed to be doing to earn the food.

Down

You can click your dog when she's lying down, but if you prefer to lure this as well, lying down is an easy progression from sitting. When she sits, either on her own or in response to your voice command, take a treat, hold it above her head, and then slowly move your hand forward and down until it's several inches in front of her. Her body will move down.

Stay

Stay can be taught from the sit, down, or stand positions. The first thing that you teach your dog to do will become her default behavior, the thing she will always do to please you when she is unsure of what she should do at any given time. People who show their dogs will teach stand and stay first because they want their dog to stand nicely for examination in the show ring. To teach your dog to stay, back away from her a bit and click her for not following you. Start with a brief second or two and gradually increase the time as well as the distance.

Come

Teaching your dog to come is simple. In fact, the entire family can get in on this one. Each person should have some treats. If you're clicker training, provide each person with a clicker as well. Call the dog and click and treat when she comes to you. Then the next person calls her and repeats the process. She'll think this is a wonderful game. Remember: never call a dog to you to yell at her or punish her. That will make her not want to join you because she'll associate your call with unpleasant experiences. There is no need for punishment with positive training. And if you use her name to call her to you for something bad, she will soon cease coming when she's called. Remember, too, not to click just to get your dog's attention when she has strayed too far. Hearing the click will probably cause her to come to you for a treat; but in the process you have actually rewarded her—clicked her—for going away from you. Instead, call her, and click when she is moving back to you, to build a stronger "Come."

Tricks of the Trade

It's important that your dog learn to walk beside you on a loose leash. She should not be chasing cats, children, bicycles, or cars, nor should she be dragging you down the road. A dog who pulls her owner down the street is not displaying good manners. You are the leader, and the experience of going for a walk should be pleasurable for you and your dog, a time of companionship and sharing, not struggle. It's easy to teach your dog to be that sort of companion. Be gentle and consistent in your training.

Walking

It may surprise you to learn that walking near you and not pulling on the leash can be taught in the house without a leash. You don't want to lure this behavior because you want her to pay attention to you, not to any treats you might be holding. Your goal is to have your dog walk quietly on your left side. Pat your left leg with your left hand as you call your dog to you. Step out with your left foot. If she comes with you, she gets a click and a treat. Be certain to stop walking before you deliver the treat. Let her concentrate on one thing at a time. She shouldn't be eating while she's walking.

If you have a small dog and don't want to keep bending over, you can use a target stick. The dog learns to touch the stick and is rewarded for that. She will soon learn to follow the stick's lead to direct her. Eventually, she will learn to associate the word of the behavior you're training with what you want her to do and you won't have to use the target stick. Like the clicker, it is phased out, then used only when you wish to teach her something new.

Your dog's training will mean few, if any, behavior problems, as well as a long, happy life as a beloved family member. Veterinarians have no problem examining a well-behaved dog, which will make trips to the animal hospital much easier for all concerned.

Canine Good Citizen Test

Every dog should be able to pass the American Kennel Club's Canine Good Citizen (CGC) test. It will show that she is a good, reliable, well-mannered dog. Your dog doesn't have to be a purebred to earn a CGC after her name. The tests are sponsored by local groups like dog clubs, community colleges, service organizations, and private training schools.

Your dog has only to demonstrate that she can accept a friendly stranger, politely sit while she's petted, walk on a loose leash, walk through a crowd, sit and lie down on command, settle down after interaction, see another dog and not overreact, and show no unusual reaction to joggers, people using wheelchairs or canes, and so on. She will also have to demonstrate that she can display good manners with a person you trust while you are out of sight. A dog who has been properly socialized will have no problem passing this portion of the test since nothing is likely to seem frightening to her and she will readily accept meeting new people.

She should be clean and neatly groomed. She will fail the test if she eliminates during the test, with one exception: if she does this during the supervised separation portion of the test when it's held outdoors. Dismissal would also come if she growled, snapped, bit someone, or attacked or attempted to attack a person or another dog.

Play Training and Competition

Once your dog has learned basic manners, you can expand this to have fun with her in an organized canine activity. Sharing activities with your dog will serve to enrich your relationship. And an active dog will stay healthier longer. Just like people, dogs need exercise.

Tricks of the Trade

Warm-ups and cooldowns are as important for dogs as they are for people. Make sure you or your instructor incorporate this sort of training, especially in the more athletic dog sports.

Obedience Trials

Obedience trials will allow you to showcase your dog's skills from the basic levels of walking and jogging at your heel and executing a proper sit, stand, and stay. If you decide to continue on, she will jump over hurdles to retrieve, then progress to scent discrimination, in which she must pick out the one item that you have touched from a group of items that look exactly alike and then bring it to you.

Agility Trials

Agility trials give you and your dog a chance to run a timed obstacle course together. The training alone, whether or not you enter a competition, is a good confidence builder for many dogs. Learning to use a teeter-totter, walk an elevated dog walk, run up an A-frame, stop to rest on command, and run through weave poles can give you and your dog a good deal of pleasure. Careful training is the key, but it's also fun.

Not all dogs and people are temperamentally suited to obedience or agility, no matter what their breed, even if it's one that's traditionally involved in these sports. Some of the newer canine sports may be better suited to you and your dog. Both obedience and agility can and should be taught with clicks and treats for good tries rather than collar yanks and reprimands for mistakes.

Flyball

Flyball is a timed team relay race. The dogs learn to run down their race lane over a series of jumps to a spring-loaded box, hit a lever that releases a tennis ball, catch the ball, and run back over the jumps to their owner. As soon as the first dog returns to her owner, the next dog on the team is off and running.

Canine Musical Freestyle

Freestyle is a choreographed dance routine with your dog. An offshoot of obedience training, it combines obedience and trick training set to music. There are two types of freestyle and two different groups. The World Canine Freestyle Organization (WCFO), which encourages mixed-breed participation as well as purebreds, puts the emphasis on bonding, sharing, and having fun with your dog. Dogs of every shape and size enjoy this sport. The routines are choreographed to show the dog and owner working together, and costumes worn by the owner reflect the music. WCFO has members around the world. There are video competitions for those who cannot get to a live competition but would still like to compete for titles. Many participants do their freestyle routines to entertain at schools and nursing homes, bringing smiles to the faces of the elderly and introducing children to a new way to have fun with their dogs. Another freestyle organization, the Canine Freestyle Federation (CFF), is also based in the United States. The routines in CFF's style of freestyle put the emphasis on the dog's movements rather than on the team of dog and owner.

Additional Activities

There are herding activities, field trials for bird dogs, hunting down tunnels for terriers, and tracking tests for dogs that were originally bred for such purposes. They enjoy having those instincts developed and working with their owners.

Some breeds of dogs are genetically programmed to be more active than others, enjoying things like flying disc competitions. And if one or more of those breeds is part of the genetic background of a mixed-breed dog, that dog, too, will need to have her energies properly channeled into an appropriate activity.

Volunteer Work

Nursing home and hospital visits are another way to have fun with your dog if she has the right temperament for it. Therapy dogs are certified for visits by organizations like The Delta Society and Therapy Dogs International, although there are also small local groups that organize therapy dog visits. You can usually find them by networking through a local dog club or your local veterinarian. After special training and the owner's commitment to regularly visit a specific facility, it's wonderfully rewarding to be able to share your special dog with others in such a meaningful way.

Tricks of the Trade

Therapy dogs touch the hearts of the people they visit. Being able to stroke a soft, warm, loving dog can provide the key that opens the door to communication for elderly people who haven't spoken in years. A therapy dog can also provide much-needed comfort for a child in pain, or any person who needs the unspoken unconditional love that a dog can provide.

There are so many choices of activities that there's something for everyone. The more you do with your dog, the closer your relationship will be, and the more fun you'll have together.

What We've Learned

Bite inhibition: The dog learns not to bite down hard

Coprophagia: Eating feces

Pica: Eating things that are indigestible

Resource guarding: The dog "protects" her property from her human, other dogs, cats, and others

Socialization: Acclimating the dog to different types of people, animals, sights, sounds, and smells so that everything in the dog's environment appears normal to the dog and the dog learns to behave in socially acceptable ways

7

Common Puppy Problems

**Responsible pet ownership pertains not only
to ensuring our pet's basic needs, such as food,
shelter, behavior training, regular veterinary care, and
love; it also includes a responsibility to eliminate the
potential for the propagation of hereditary disease.
The eradication of genetic diseases in domestic
animals through selective breeding is our choice!**
—Paul C. Gambardella, V.M.D.,
M.S., Diplomate, A.C.V.S.

Everyone who acquires a puppy anticipates a long, happy, healthy life for that little one. Sadly, not every puppy will be healthy.

If you've acquired your puppy from a breeder, you should always ask to see the health clearances for the puppy's parents. Clearance from the Orthopedic Foundation for Animals (OFA) for hip and elbow dysplasia (or PennHip index for hip joint laxity) and clearance from the Canine Eye Research Foundation (CERF) for genetic eye problems such as progressive retinal atrophy will assure you that the breeder is trying to eliminate these problems from the line. And don't be afraid to ask about other genetic problems that are particular to the breed and what the breeder is doing to eliminate those. Ethical, responsible breeders use every possible genetic test before breeding to determine whether the dogs they want to breed are free of defects that could be passed along to future generations.

What happens if your puppy is diagnosed with a genetic physical problem? That depends on the problem and its severity. Here we'll discuss some of the more common genetic problems.

Umbilical Hernia

An umbilical hernia occurs when a bit of the abdominal contents protrudes through the abdominal wall at the umbilicus (belly button) without coming through the skin. It occurs when the umbilical ring doesn't close completely. Not all umbilical hernias need to be repaired, but when they are large enough to allow intestine to pass through the hole, surgery is needed. Hernias are easily reducible and can be repaired while the dog is undergoing an elective surgery such as spaying or neutering. Umbilical hernias are considered genetic. It is recommended that these dogs not be bred, even after the hernia has been repaired.

Orthopedic Diseases

Orthopedic diseases are those that affect the bones and joints. Depending on their severity, they can cause great pain and discomfort for your dog.

Hip Dysplasia

The word *dysplasia* means abnormal development. Hip dysplasia causes debilitating lameness. While it is commonly thought of as a problem for larger dogs, it can affect very small dogs too. First diagnosed in the 1930s, hip dysplasia is caused by a laxity in the hip joint that prevents the ball at the top of the thigh bone from fitting tightly into the socket in the hip. The loose fit of the ball-and-socket joint causes the ball to move in and out of the socket, which is a form of trauma. The trauma causes inflammation and damage to the joint, leading to osteoarthritis, also known as degenerative joint disease (DJD).

Unfortunately, many dogs who have hip dysplasia don't always show obvious signs of the disease, such as pain or lameness. In those cases it is diagnosed by traditional radiography, or a PennHip (University of Pennsylvania Hip Improvement Program) index to determine hip joint laxity. The traditional x-ray may not reveal degenerative changes until the dog is two years old, but the PennHip index can be used in much younger dogs.

Dogs that show outward signs of hip dysplasia may be reluctant to go upstairs, though going down is not a problem. They can also develop a "bunny-hop" gait in the rear legs as they run. Young, otherwise healthy dogs will seem to tire quickly and want to lie down to rest in the middle of exercising; they will also seem very tired at the end of the day, and remain lying down longer than a normal dog. Sometimes when an owner touches the hip area, the dog will growl or whimper in anticipation of being hurt. These are all signs that there is pain in the hip joints, and a veterinarian should examine the dog in order to determine the cause.

The hip joint cannot be returned to a normal state once DJD has begun, but there are surgical procedures available to make a dog more comfortable, such as total hip replacement. This is the same surgery that is done in humans who have irreversible hip pain, whereby both the ball and socket are replaced with prostheses. This surgery is not recommended for puppies because their immature and growing bone is not ready for a prosthesis; it is intended to help adult dogs with mature skeletons. Young dogs may benefit from a triple pelvic osteotomy (TPO), which changes the position of the socket so that the ball does not move in and out of the socket, thereby greatly minimizing the inevitable DJD. The best results are obtained when this surgery is performed before the DJD has begun— usually between six and twelve months of age.

The symptoms of DJD are variable, but all point to pain. Some cases of hip dysplasia cannot be diagnosed until the dog is two years of age, but dogs that have clinical signs of the disease can be diagnosed as early as four to six months, and then the veterinarian can determine whether surgery will be beneficial. In mild cases (those that may not be diagnosed until the dog is two years of age) the dog will probably not need surgery until perhaps later in life when the DJD is bad—but it may never become bad enough to warrant surgery. If you suspect a problem, see your veterinarian.

Another available surgery is the femoral head and neck excision, which is alternately called a femoral head ostectomy (FHO) or an excision arthroplasty. This older procedure was used in humans before total hip replacements became available. The ball of the joint is removed and the dog eventually forms a joint made from scar tissue. Most patients are relieved of pain and acquire good to excellent mobility after a few months of walking exercise. It's usually performed on younger dogs who are mobile but experiencing pain in one or both hip joints. The procedure has faster results in smaller dogs but can also be performed on large dogs. The FHO is generally reserved for dogs under seventy-five pounds as their fully grown adult weight, but the philosophy of the individual surgeon enters into this decision.

The FHO has not been successful in the Giant breeds, such as the St. Bernard, Great Dane, and Newfoundland. Physical therapy is more difficult to accomplish in very heavy dogs, and the Giant breeds are usually over a hundred pounds. There are new physical therapy techniques, such

RELIEVING THE PAIN

Medication, such as nonsteroidal anti-inflammatory drugs (NSAIDs), may be suggested by your veterinarian to reduce pain and inflammation. NSAIDs may cause abdominal irritation and should be used only under your veterinarian's watchful eye in a carefully prescribed dose. Never use ibuprofen, as it can be fatal to your dog. Use a buffered aspirin or children's aspirin, but only under your veterinarian's supervision.

as the use of underwater treadmills, that may increase the success rate in the Giant breeds, but these techniques are not available everywhere.

If the dog experiences a flare-up of the problem after any of these corrective surgeries are performed, your veterinarian may choose to limit exercise or recommend swimming as an option, because it is a non–weight-bearing activity.

Alternative medicine should not be used before an accurate diagnosis is made. However, after that point it may be beneficial to supplement traditional medicine with alternative medicine. Nutraceuticals such as glucosamine and chondroitin certainly have a place in treatment. They don't cure anything, but they offer a great help in the control of pain.

Elbow Dysplasia

The term *elbow dysplasia* describes DJD of the elbow joints caused by one or more congenital problems that can affect the elbows. These conditions are hereditary, and they can usually be diagnosed definitively by x-ray before the dog is one year of age. Depending on the specific condition, surgery may be helpful in reducing the pain; however, DJD is inevitable in all cases, regardless of surgery. Obesity can exacerbate any joint problem, which is one more reason to maintain a healthy weight for your dog through diet and gentle exercise. Applications of heat or cold to the affected joint may help ease pain. Nutraceuticals such as glucosamine and chondroitin may also be suggested by your veterinarian to supplement care and treatment. Always check with your veterinarian before using dietary supplements.

Luxating Patella

A luxating patella is like a "trick knee"—the patella, or kneecap, pops out of place. The patella is a floating bone within the tendon of the quadriceps muscle. It resides in the groove (*trochlea*) at the lower end of the femur, gliding over the trochlea as the knee joint is extended and flexed. If it pops out toward the inside of the leg, it's called a *medial*

Tricks of the Trade

The anatomic directional terms *lateral* and *medial* refer to a portion of the body that is either away from (lateral) or toward (medial) the midline of the body. People stand upright, creating a front and a back—in anatomic directional language the front is referred to as *anterior* and the back is referred to as *posterior*. In the case of quadrupeds (our four-legged friends), the front points toward the head and the back points toward the tail, so the front is referred to as *cranial* and the back is referred to as *caudal*.

luxating patella, and if it pops toward the outside, it's called a *lateral luxating patella*.

In some cases this condition can result in arthritis. In 1968, researcher John William Putnam theorized that a bad angle of the hip joint exerts a force down the leg, and as the leg grows the kneecap is pulled out of place—therefore a normal groove doesn't develop, allowing the patella to easily pop out. With the rare exception of trauma cases, a luxating patella is a hereditary condition.

There are four clinical grades of luxating patella that help veterinarians describe the severity of the problem. A Grade I usually causes an occasional hopping. The patella remains in place most of the time but can be pushed out by the veterinarian during examination. It doesn't have to be repaired unless it worsens, and it may never worsen. This grade of luxation is mild and doesn't always mean that the joint will become arthritic.

A Grade II patella pops in and out, and you can see the dog extend his leg in order to pop the kneecap back into place. Dogs with Grade II patella luxations usually need surgery. Grade II can lead to arthritis.

Grade III means that the patella is always out of place but the dog can still bear weight and the kneecap can be pushed back into place by the examiner. Surgery will be necessary as soon as possible, especially if the dog is young and still growing.

Grade IV is the most severe—the patella is permanently out of place and the dog has a difficult time bearing weight on that leg. Although surgery is recommended, it isn't always successful with a Grade IV patella luxation.

Luxating patellas aren't usually painful, but they cause a mechanical lameness that is a nuisance for the dog. Toy breeds with Grade III or IV luxations in both back legs usually do not use the back legs at all. The dog will walk on his front legs, lifting both hind legs off the ground, if both legs are affected. As the years pass, painful arthritis can set in.

Legg-Calve-Perthes Disease

Legg-Calve-Perthes disease, otherwise simply known as Legg-Perthes, is an uncommon orthopedic problem that usually affects smaller dogs (usually males under twenty-five pounds). It's a hereditary disease that affects the hip. Doctors Legg, Calve, and Perthes first described this condition in children, but it was Dr. Gerry Schnelle, a former Angell Memorial Animal Hospital chief of staff, who was the first to report it in the dog.

In Legg-Perthes disease, the blood supply toward the top of the femur is cut off, resulting in the loss of blood to the bone and ultimately death of the bone (*avascular necrosis*). Between four and eight months of age the dog will begin displaying symptoms, such as a limp or a hop on one or both rear legs. Unfortunately, by the time a veterinarian sees the puppy and makes the diagnosis, the condition can't be reversed because degeneration of the hip joint has already occurred. The only effective treatment is to perform a FHO, which removes the ball (head of the femur) and allows a new joint to form out of scar tissue. Some dogs will end up with a mild limp, but the surgery eliminates the pain.

Panosteitis

Panosteitis is seen in large dogs and usually emerges when the dog is between five and twenty-four months of age, although it has been seen in puppies as young as two months and adults as old as seven years. The disease affects the long bones in the body (radius, ulna, humerus, femur, and tibia); applying digital pressure to the affected bones will elicit a painful response during an examination. (*Digital pressure* refers to using one's fingers to apply pressure directly on the bone through the skin.) We really have no idea how it feels to the dog, because dogs cannot talk, but we do know that it hurts because they cry out or act pained in other recognizable ways. X-rays are used to confirm the diagnosis.

Tricks of the Trade

The radius and ulna are the two bones that make up the forearm of the dog or human— from the wrist to the elbow. The humerus is the bone that makes up the upper arm from the elbow to the shoulder. The femur is also known as the thigh bone, and it connects the hip with the knee. The tibia is the main bone that connects the knee with the ankle. These are referred to as the long bones of the body.

The pain typically moves from one leg to the other and then disappears, only to return, which makes diagnosis difficult. Veterinarians refer to this as a *shifting leg lameness*. The pain can last for a month or two and treatment usually involves aspirin or a similar drug. Corticosteroids can be prescribed for severe cases. Ultimately the condition will disappear, with or without treatment, because it is a self-limiting disease.

Respiratory Ailments

Respiratory ailments can be very dangerous, as they interfere with your dog's breathing function. You must take great care to treat these conditions, and prevent them when possible, for the sake of your dog's health and longevity.

Collapsing Trachea

Collapsing trachea affects nearly all of the toy breeds—if they don't have it, they probably are predisposed to the condition. This does not mean that all dogs of toy breeding are affected; it means that individual dogs in all of the toy breeds *can* be affected. We know that the condition is hereditary, but because we don't know the mode of inheritance or the identity of the gene we cannot predict the outcome of breeding affected dogs.

This respiratory disease exists when the trachea (the *windpipe*—the tube made of cartilage rings leading from the neck to the chest that carries air to the lungs) is weakened and the rings flatten and air is cut off. The dog will show symptoms as early as birth, but symptoms may not appear until the dog is more than five years old. The symptoms include shortness of breath, fatigue, and coughing. Often the dog appears to be unable to catch his breath and seems somewhat frightened. The harder the dog tries to cough or breathe, the more the problem is aggravated.

Secondhand smoke exacerbates the problem, as does reacting with alarm when the dog has an attack or trying too hard to reassure the dog. It is best to remain calm, and be sure the dog is in a cool and stress-free environment. If the labored breathing worsens or continues for hours, then you must seek veterinary care. The dog may need medication and/or an oxygen-enriched environment until the crisis passes.

Your veterinarian will be able to give a prognosis depending on the extent of the tracheal involvement. Some dogs may benefit from surgery.

Elongated Soft Palate

Elongated soft palate is an anatomical anomaly that occurs when the soft palate (the loose tissue just past the roof of the mouth) is unusually long. When this occurs, the elongated soft palate can block the glottis (entryway into the trachea), and even enter the glottis, when the dog tries to inhale air. A loud snoring noise may occur. It is a common problem in brachycephalic breeds (for example, Bulldogs, Boston Terriers, Boxers) and can seriously interfere with breathing. Surgical removal of the elongated portion of the soft palate is the treatment of choice. The surgical laser is often used for this procedure to more easily control hemorrhage.

Stenotic Nares

Stenotic nares are associated with brachycephalic breeds such as the Pug and Brussels Griffon. It's often diagnosed when the puppy visits the veterinarian for the first time for initial vaccinations. This is another problem that causes the affected dog to have difficulty inspiring air—this time through the nostrils. The nostrils (*nares*) develop with a very small opening, and the act of inspiration can actually close the nostrils even further. Correcting the problem involves trimming the lateral nostril flap in order to create a wider opening. It's a simple surgical procedure.

Cardiac Diseases

Diseases of the heart and circulatory system can obviously have a tremendous impact on your dog's life, from limiting activity and diet to requiring expensive medications. As with respiratory diseases, it's vital that you proactively monitor your dog's health, treating any conditions that arise and preventing conditions when possible.

Congenital Heart Disease

Congenital heart disease refers to a group of hereditary diseases that are created by anatomical defects of the heart and/or major vessels of the heart. Two common examples are patent ductus arteriosus and pulmonic stenosis.

Patent Ductus Arteriosus (PDA). Patent ductus arteriosus (PDA or *shunt*) is a vessel that connects the aorta to the pulmonary artery in the fetus. When the puppy is in utero, the vessel is normally open (patent) and functioning before birth to divert blood from going into the nonfunctional lungs. As soon as the puppy is born and the lungs start functioning, the ductus arteriosus closes and becomes no longer open (patent). Therefore, a PDA in the born puppy is abnormal because if the shunt doesn't close, double and triple loads of blood go to one side of the heart, ultimately causing heart failure. PDA can be surgically corrected. The surgery should be performed as soon as possible in order to avoid congestive heart failure. Most dogs can live a normal lifespan following surgery. PDA should be discovered at the first veterinary visit and initial vaccination.

Pulmonic Stenosis. Pulmonic stenosis is an abnormally small passageway in the pulmonary artery (the vessel that carries blood from the heart to the lungs). This causes the right side of the heart to work too hard trying to pump enough blood to the lungs for oxygenation, causing heart failure. Depending on the severity of the problem, some dogs can be treated successfully for many years with medication—however, others may need surgical correction. Consultation with a veterinary cardiologist is advisable for each individual case.

Portosystemic Shunt

Portosystemic shunt, also known as liver shunt, is the most common congenital liver problem seen in young puppies. Blood is supposed to go from the intestines through the portal vein and into the liver before it enters the heart to be circulated through the entire body. In the case of a portosystemic shunt, the blood is "shunted" from the intestines directly to the veins leading to the heart, bypassing the liver. This causes a buildup of toxins in the body that the liver normally detoxifies. Stunted growth, weight loss, seizures, persistent vomiting, and diarrhea are the signs associated with this condition. Unfortunately, in some cases diagnosis can be difficult. The best treatment is to surgically close down the shunt and force the blood to circulate through the liver. The success of the surgery depends on the integrity of the blood vessels in the liver and the location of the shunt. Surgery is not always successful.

Von Willebrand's Disease

Von Willebrand's Disease (vWD) is a congenital bleeding disorder in which the dog's blood doesn't effectively clot, and excessive bleeding occurs as a result of trauma or surgery. Female dogs will also have post-partum bleeding. All breeds in which this disorder is known to occur (Doberman Pinscher, Jack Russell Terrier, Miniature Schnauzer, German Shepherd, and Rottweiler) should be tested for the disease before any thought is given to breeding. Since the disease is hereditary, females with vWD should not be bred, not only due to the risk of postpartum bleeding, but because they could pass the condition on to their offspring.

Ophthalmologic Diseases

Ophthalmology refers to the study and care of the eyes. Unfortunately, your dog's vision can be impaired by any number of conditions.

Progressive Retinal Atrophy (PRA)

Progressive retinal atrophy (PRA) is a degenerative condition of the back of the eye (retina) that leads to blindness. The disease most closely resembles retinitis pigmentosa in humans. The disease begins as night blindness—the dog has difficulty seeing in dim light and the owner may notice the dog bumping into furniture in dimly lit conditions. It has an early onset in some breeds, such as the Miniature Schnauzer, Collie, and Irish Setter. Diagnosis is made by ophthalmoscope (the instrument used to see the lesions on the retina; it contains a perforated mirror and lenses) or by electroretinography (the process of recording the electrical activity that occurs when the retina is stimulated with light).

Juvenile Cataracts

Juvenile cataracts is an early-onset condition. Diagnosed by a biomicroscope (which enables the ophthalmologist to see the cataract), it is the opacity of the ocular lens or the capsule in which it's held that creates the condition. Juvenile cataracts causes blindness and there is no known cure at this time, although research into the condition is ongoing. When the dog becomes blind, the lens can be removed to allow for some vision.

Entropion

Entropion is a congenital condition in which the eyelid turns inward and rubs against the eye. It's usually the lower eyelid that turns inward, but in some breeds the upper eyelid can do this as well. This causes the eyelashes to rub against the cornea, which then causes the dog to blink since he's uncomfortable. The blinking causes more scraping of the eyelashes over the cornea, thus exacerbating the problem. Entropion must be surgically corrected as soon as possible to avoid further damage to the cornea. If the dog isn't treated, there can be infection, corneal ulcers, and, at the very least, painful, watery eyes. Commonly seen in the Shar-Pei, it's also seen in the Bulldog, Bloodhound, and Chow.

Neurological Problems

The two most common neurological problems that can occur in puppies are hydrocephalus and canine distemper. We discussed canine distemper in Chapter 1.

Hydrocephalus

Hydrocephalus comes from *hydro*, meaning "water," and *cephalus*, meaning "brain." It's not quite water on the brain, but that's fairly close to being accurate. On rare occasions it is due to an infection of the brain early in life, or to some other problem in the brain that cannot be identified. It's a hereditary condition (in most cases) in which the ventricles of the brain are stretched because there's a blockage (obstruction) of the cerebrospinal fluid pathways. This causes an accumulation of cerebrospinal fluid in the skull. However, in some of the most severe cases the head does not enlarge at all. The brain can shrink (atrophy), and there can be mental deterioration and convulsions. It can, eventually, even lead to death. In severe cases surgery can be done to permanently drain the excess fluid from the brain to the abdominal cavity to correct the problem. Hydrocephalus is a common condition in most toy breeds and, in fact, there are few Chihuahuas that aren't hydrocephalic to one degree or another. Chihuahua breeders consider a mild form of it to be normal.

What We've Learned

Dysplasia: Abnormal development

Glottis: The entryway to the trachea

Nares: Nostrils

Orthopedic diseases: Diseases that affect the bones and joints

Osteoarthritis: Degenerative joint disease (DJD)

Trochlea: The groove at the lower end of the femur

8

Routine Surgery and Anesthesia

Anesthesia and surgery go hand in hand.
Cutting into live tissue (surgery) is painful, and
to prevent the patient from feeling the pain both
during and after surgery, an anesthetic and an
analgesic (pain reliever) must be given. Just as newer
and better surgical procedures are being developed at a
rapid pace to treat disease, injury, and deformity, so, too,
are the art and science of anesthesia advancing at the
same rapid rate—anesthesia has never been safer.
The result of the surgeon's work depends entirely on
the patient's ability to heal. Only through good
anesthesia and analgesia coupled with skillful surgical
technique can the potential to heal be maximized.
— *Paul C. Gambardella, V.M.D.,*
M.S., Diplomate, A.C.V.S.

It should be expected that your dog will have to undergo routine surgery at some point in his life. Surgery will mean that your dog will have to be anesthetized. Anesthesia is also usually necessary for a routine dental cleaning. This chapter will give you an appreciation and understanding of what to expect when your dog requires anesthesia and surgery—including a discussion of the most common surgery your dog is likely to face, spaying or neutering. You should feel comfortable talking with your veterinarian about all aspects of your dog's care, including those related to surgery.

Routine surgery includes:

- A preliminary visit with the veterinarian to learn about the procedure
- Bloodwork
- Anesthesia
- Specific medications (such as anesthetics, sedatives, or antibiotics) that will be given
- Drugs
- Instructions for postoperative care
- Followup checkups

Bloodwork

Taking blood from a patient before surgery will tell the surgeon who is going to perform the procedure exactly what the dog's condition is prior to surgery, including kidney and liver functions. This will help your veterinarian decide which anesthetic agents are going to be the best ones to use on that particular dog under those particular circumstances. This is the same bloodwork that is done on humans prior to surgery.

There are two common types of blood tests. One is a *CBC* (*complete blood count*), which measures the number of red and white cells in the blood. A low blood count, also known as *anemia*, can be caused by a multitude of diseases and conditions. A few of the most common are kidney disease, blood loss, gastric ulceration, and parasites. The second test is a *chemistry panel*, or *chem screen*. The chemistry panel measures different substances produced or regulated by the internal organs, such as electrolytes (like sodium and potassium), glucose, enzymes, and even waste products that will be excreted through the kidneys.

Anesthesia

All licensed veterinarians, or the technicians under their supervision, can administer anesthesia to your pet. The technicians who are trained to administer anesthesia are referred to as *anesthetists*. They are also responsible for the close monitoring of the anesthetized patients. It is their job to keep the patient stable under a sufficient plane of anesthesia to allow the procedure to be performed. Respiration rate, heart rate and rhythm, blood

WHEN YOU NEED A SPECIALIST

Veterinary anesthesiology is a specialty of its own, and whenever your dog's condition places her at a high risk for a complication occurring as a result of anesthesia, your veterinarian may refer you to a specialty practice or institution where a veterinary anesthesiologist can determine the protocol. There are currently approximately one hundred fifty veterinarians board certified by the American College of Veterinary Anesthesiologists (ACVA) in the world. The vast majority of these anesthesiologists are working at universities (in schools and colleges of veterinary medicine) or large private hospitals like Angell Memorial.

oxygen content, and body temperature are among the vital statistics that are monitored in patients under anesthesia. The anesthetist ensures that all functions are normal and intervenes if complications arise.

It is standard procedure to recommend that animals fast twelve to twenty-four hours prior to anesthesia. Fasting will keep the stomach empty and decrease the likelihood of regurgitation (passive vomiting) under anesthesia. If regurgitated stomach contents were to be inhaled, or *aspirated*, aspiration pneumonia could result, which is a very serious problem. It is also beneficial to have an empty stomach so that the diaphragm can move freely and allow the patient to take full, deep breaths.

The anesthetic protocol to be used on a patient depends on many factors, including the dog's health and general condition, the type and duration of the procedure, and even the personal preference of your veterinarian. Normally, your dog will first receive an intravenous agent that induces anesthesia (that is, causes her to fall asleep rapidly), then an anesthetic gas that she breathes to maintain the anesthesia. In order to administer the gas, a tube is placed into the trachea (windpipe), a process called *intubation*.

Risks

While under anesthesia, dogs will not blink their eyes, and this can cause the corneas to dry out. Therefore, the dog's eyes are lubricated during surgery to prevent dryness and possible corneal ulceration.

All dogs are at risk of developing acute kidney (*renal*) failure and dehydration as a result of anesthesia unless fluids are given intravenously during the procedure. When a dog breathes through her nasal passages, the air she takes in is humidified by the mucosa that lines the breathing passages. But because air travels through a tube and not the nose while the dog is intubated, the air is not humidified. This is the reason that intravenous fluid administration has become standard procedure in all anesthetized patients, since animals need to remain well hydrated in order for their kidneys to function properly.

For a variety of reasons, a dog's heart can stop beating while she is under anesthesia. When this happens, blood stops circulating between the heart and lungs. This is known as *cardiac arrest*, and it means that both the heart and lungs have stopped functioning. Dogs undergoing elective surgery are at a very low risk of having a cardiac arrest, because they are usually in good general health. Your veterinarian will tell you if your dog is in a higher risk category. All AAHA-accredited hospitals (see page 143) are required to have rescuscitative equipment close by in order to properly treat a cardiac arrest.

Respiratory failure (breathing too slowly or shallowly for adequate oxygenation of the blood to occur in the lungs) is more common than cardiac arrest during anesthesia. This is in part because inhaled anesthetics depress the respiratory system, causing the patient to breathe less deeply and less frequently. Occasionally, a dog will stop breathing altogether (this is known as *respiratory arrest*) and will need assisted or controlled ventilation.

Special Considerations

Many owners and breeders are convinced by anecdotal experience or rumors that their breed is extremely sensitive to anesthesia. In most cases this is not so, though exceptions exist. Sighthounds—Greyhounds, Whippets, Afghans, and Borzoi—are definitely more sensitive to anesthetic agents. It has been shown that these breeds metabolize the barbiturates differently, and the relatively low ratio of body fat to muscle contributes to their slower recovery rates. When proper precautions are taken, these breeds can be anesthetized as safely as other breeds of comparable body condition and health status. Your veterinarian will choose the drug protocol with care whenever a member of this group requires anesthesia.

If your dog had a bad reaction or experience during a previous anesthetic episode, you should let your veterinarian know. A copy of the previous medical record, or direct communication from the previous veterinarian, is ideal. This can help to avoid a problem.

Very small dogs lose body heat more rapidly than larger dogs, so the anesthetist must ensure that little dogs are kept warm. This is usually done with circulating warm water heating pads.

Dogs that are very sick or severely injured will not only require special consideration regarding the anesthetic agents and monitoring, but may also need critical care follow-up for several hours or days. If your veterinarian does not provide long-term critical care, she may refer you to a hospital that has a critical care unit.

Brachycephalic dogs also present an anesthetic challenge. All parts of the upper airway in these breeds are smaller than those of other breeds of similar size. There are five conditions associated with the upper airway that collectively are termed *brachycephalic syndrome*: *stenotic nares*, which means the nostrils are smaller than normal; *extra tissue in the nares*; *hypoplastic trachea*, which means the windpipe is smaller in diameter than normal; *everted vocal folds*, which tend to narrow the opening to the windpipe; and *elongated soft palate*, meaning the soft palate can obstruct the opening to the windpipe (the *glottis*). Though brachycephalic breeds are able to breathe through the tube once it's inserted and they handle the anesthetic drugs very well, their anatomic anomalies can make it difficult to insert the tube, and can also cause a problem for the dog immediately following removal of the tube during recovery from anesthesia. In order to avoid these complications, a skillful anesthetist or your veterinarian should do the intubating, and the tube should be left in place longer than normal during the recovery phase and until the patient has fully regained her swallowing reflex. This may take several minutes longer.

The Toy breeds with collapsing trachea might also be expected to pose a problem, but an experienced anesthetist usually intubates with ease. The endotracheal tube actually holds open the collapsing trachea during anesthesia.

Senior dogs must have their age taken into account when they're anesthetized. Like humans, dogs' body systems slow down with age; metabolism slows down; they don't eat as much; they need more sleep; and they need less anesthesia. Anesthesia taxes all body systems. Diseases may come with age—for example, liver or kidney disease—and they can remain hidden from the owner. Your veterinarian will probably insist on more extensive laboratory tests prior to anesthesia if your dog is elderly.

Surgery

The American Animal Hospital Association (AAHA) is the group that accredits veterinary hospitals. AAHA-approved hospitals are found throughout the United States and Canada. In order to receive accreditation, hospitals are required to meet AAHA's standards for services and facilities in twelve specific areas. This means that according to AAHA, the hospital and veterinarians have "a unique commitment to the highest standards of veterinary care as well as concern for preventive medicine." Trained AAHA practice consultants periodically visit animal hospitals and do thorough evaluations, called *surveys*, to confirm that the facilities comply with AAHA standards.

There are three levels of accreditation: two-year, three-year, and four-year. This tiered system acknowledges that not every hospital has the resources available to compete with larger facilities, but encourages everyone who strives for excellence to participate in the program.

The requirements for approval by AAHA are stringent in order to assure pet owners of the highest standard of care. The hospital must be orderly and keep adequate medical records for each patient so that there is a continuity of care. The hospital must have complete diagnostic facilities, which includes examination rooms, radiology services, clinical pathology services, and the equipment necessary to provide comprehensive inpatient and outpatient services. The hospital must be fully equipped to make prompt, accurate diagnosis and treatment. An onsite library of basic textbooks and current periodicals is also required. The veterinary hospital must have complete pharmacy facilities perpetually stocked with the most frequently used medicines. Controlled substances must be monitored, and clients must be adequately informed concerning treatment.

During surgery, the hospital must use proper anesthetic procedures, which include conducting a pre-anesthetic examination before surgery.

The hospital must provide safe, painless, state-of-the-art anesthesia during surgery. The hospital must use aseptic (free from infection) surgical technique. There are very strict requirements regarding the sterilization of equipment, including how one monitors to verify the effectiveness of the sterilization process. If, for example, steam sterilization, which is the most common, is used, there are guidelines outlining the pressure and the temperature that must be used for a specific period of time to ensure proper sterilization.

The AAHA hospital must have a single-use room for surgery with proper lighting, sterile equipment, and easy access to drugs and equipment. Nothing else can be done in that room except surgery. (This is a departure from the old days, when almost anything would be done anywhere in an animal hospital.) Today's animal hospital is quite similar to a human hospital. There are specific preparations required for the doctors and the patient. All support staff, as well as the surgeon and the anesthetist, must wear sterile gloves, cap, mask, and gown during each procedure. A different pack must be used for each procedure. Just as in a human hospital, they must "scrub in" before performing surgery. While this would appear to be common sense, it is nevertheless spelled out so there is no mistaking the intent that every procedure is performed under the best possible circumstances.

At the four-year level of accreditation, every patient who is presented for surgery must have a documented presurgical examination immediately prior to the procedure. The veterinarian will verify what's normal and abnormal for every system in the dog's body. In other words, even if the dog is going in for a spaying, which is a very common and routine procedure, preoperative testing (appropriate for the age and health status), proper aseptic surgical technique, and appropriate anesthetic protocol is used as though it were a nonroutine, major surgical procedure. This is not to alarm the client. This should, in fact, assure the client that all proper care is being taken for every surgical procedure.

There are requirements regarding support equipment, including equipment to do CPR, which might be necessary in the case of an anesthetic emergency. While there's seldom a need for it, it's critically important that the equipment is available when it is needed. Blood pressure monitoring is now much more common in veterinary medicine, and the equipment will likely become a requirement in all veterinary surgical rooms in the near future since blood pressure monitoring is considered important under anesthesia.

Nursing care is a vital part of an efficient animal hospital. Skilled veterinary technicians provide invaluable support since they contribute immensely to the professional care pets receive, from diagnosis through recuperation.

Safe and sanitary conditions must be maintained throughout the veterinary hospital, from the reception room to the kennel, including the outside premises. Each AAHA hospital must provide, or have access to, twenty-four–hour emergency service for its clients.

Dental service is also considered an important part of an AAHA hospital since oral hygiene is as important to a pet's health as it is to a human's health. AAHA hospitals routinely perform teeth cleaning, extractions, and gum work.

All AAHA hospitals meet or exceed these standards for facilities, equipment, and quality procedures. The AAHA standards are revised periodically to ensure that all animal hospitals are functioning at their optimum level and to keep raising the bar of excellence within the profession. AAHA is continually looking to upgrade the quality of care in animal hospitals.

Postoperative Treatment

Pain relief is a very important part of operative and postoperative care. It has only been during the past ten years that veterinarians have been able to scientifically determine that animals feel pain, though they might not show it in a way we recognize, so a greater emphasis is placed on pain management today than ever before.

A wide selection of pain-relieving drugs (*analgesics*) are available to dogs. Most veterinary practices use opiate analgesics (such as morphine) to relieve pain. A veterinarian's choice of analgesic will vary depending on the age, size, level of pain, and condition of the patient. A young, healthy dog would probably require a higher dose of an analgesic, while an older, sicker dog would need less to get the same effect.

Don't confuse analgesics with tranquilizers—they are not the same. Analgesics relieve pain, while tranquilizers (such as Valium) sedate but do not relieve pain. Some narcotics cause sedation as well as pain relief. Most veterinarians will talk with you about the use of pain-relieving medications before your dog is admitted for surgery—if not, then you should ask about it. It will be comforting to know that everything possible will be done to minimize the pain associated with the surgery.

Your veterinarian or a knowledgeable member of the hospital's health care team will give you specific instructions for postoperative home care. Most hospitals also include written instructions that tell you what to expect when observing the incision; the care of a bandage; dietary and/or exercise restrictions, if any; the administration of medications (topical or oral); and when to return for reexamination and suture removal. Your instructions will include an invitation to call the hospital if you have any questions. Always take advantage of this, and never let a question go unanswered!

Spaying and Neutering

The most common surgical procedures are spaying and neutering—the surgical removal of the reproductive organs for a female and male, respectively. Both are easily accomplished in the very young puppy but can be done at any time in the dog's life. The earlier the surgery is performed, however, the more likely it is that it will help prevent certain cancers and undesirable behavioral characteristics from developing. In the case of males, the threat of testicular cancer is completely eliminated. And in a female spayed before the first heat period, the incidence of breast cancer is also eliminated. Other common problems that are prevented by spaying and neutering include prostate gland disease, uterine infections, and tumors around the anus in older male dogs (*perianal adenomas*).

At approximately six months of age, when male puppies begin sexual maturation, they will begin to mark, and they may become aggressive, roam, and exhibit mounting behavior. Neutering can help prevent these problems.

Tricks of the Trade

In some cases, especially in breeds at risk or with a family history of torsion, it would be a good idea to fasten the stomach to the abdominal wall while a spaying or other abdominal surgery is being performed so that if the dog bloats later in life there won't also be torsion. Discuss this with your veterinarian.

A pediatric spaying or neutering (spaying or neutering between six and twelve weeks of age), providing the veterinarian is comfortable with anesthetizing and operating on very young dogs, can be done safely and without complications. This procedure is usually reserved for humane organizations and shelters in order to be able to send puppies to their new homes after ensuring that they are unable to reproduce. Many responsible breeders are also spaying and neutering their pet-quality puppies before sending them to their new homes to assure that they will not be bred.

It is best to follow your veterinarian's advice regarding the timing of spaying or neutering. Unless you intend to breed the dog, it is the policy at Angell Memorial Animal Hospital to recommend spaying or neutering at the time of your puppy's last vaccination (approximately four months of age). During the past ten years scientific research has taken place to determine whether there are undesirable physical or behavioral problems later in life following a pediatric spaying or neutering. Thus far, no undesirable effects have been found. Spaying and neutering is the same for older dogs as it is for younger ones, but younger dogs heal faster. However, the anesthetic protocol is a little more involved for the pediatric canine patient. The pediatric anesthetic protocol for both puppies and kittens was developed at Angell Memorial and published nearly ten years ago. These guidelines have proven to be very safe for these patients.

Some people believe that it is healthier to spay a female after she has had a litter or to neuter a male after he has reached full physical maturity. There is no scientific evidence to support these beliefs. Unless you are planning to enter your dog in shows or breed the dog, the best time for spaying or neutering is after the final puppy vaccination.

The medical term for spaying is *ovariohysterectomy* (OHE), and the term for neutering a male is *castration* (removal of the testicles). Even though they are both considered routine elective surgical procedures, performed by virtually all family veterinarians, they are also treated as major surgical procedures with regard to anesthetic protocol and aseptic technique.

The OHE in the female is the complete removal of both ovaries and the entire uterus, usually excluding the cervix. If any portion of an ovary is remaining, the dog will continue to have heat periods; if any portion of the uterus is left, it will be susceptible to infection. The major arteries and veins that enter and leave the ovaries and uterus are tied off with suture material or metal clips (*ligated*), which prevents blood from passing through the vessels. The abdominal cavity is then sutured closed.

The castration of a male dog does not require entrance into a major body cavity unless one or both testicles have not descended from the abdominal cavity into the scrotum. Both testicles will descend into the scrotum before birth in normal dogs. The surgical procedure to neuter a male dog usually involves making one small (between one and two inches) incision just in front of the scrotum. Both testicles (one at a time) are forced through the one incision by the surgeon and removed. The spermatic cords, consisting of the sperm ducts and major vessels that supply blood to the testicles, are ligated in order to separate them from the testicles. The incision is then closed with suture material.

Some veterinarians will allow patients that have been spayed or neutered to go home on the same day, depending on how early the procedure was performed and the condition of the patient. Some veterinarians like to keep them overnight and send them home the next day.

For the next two weeks, you will need to keep your dog in the house, except for short leash walks in order to get some exercise and for eliminating. When there are sutures to be removed, you will need to take your dog back to the veterinarian, usually about ten days later. Some veterinarians use sutures that dissolve and therefore do not need to be removed.

What We've Learned

Analgesic: A pain-relieving drug

Anemia: Low blood count

Aseptic: Free from infection

Ligate: Tie off a vessel with suture material or a metal clip

Neutering: Surgery performed on males that removes the testicles

OHE: Medical term for spaying

Spaying: Surgery performed on females; the complete removal of both ovaries and the entire uterus

Trachea: Windpipe

PART II

The Middle Years

9

The Annual Checkup

The annual examination is your opportunity
to update your veterinarian with all of your
observations, which will help guide this visit.
The goal is to do all the important things to keep
your pet healthy—it is a team effort that matches
the owner's valuable personal experience with
the expertise of your veterinarian.
— *Peter Theran, V.M.D.,*
Diplomate, A.C.V.I.M.

It's important that your middle-aged dog be examined annually, just the way you would have a routine physical examination done by your own physician. The old adage that an ounce of prevention is worth a pound of cure has never held more true than it does today. It is less expensive, less time-consuming, and less stressful to prevent an illness than it is to cure it. And to catch an illness in the early stages can make it much easier to treat. Scheduling an annual veterinary visit for your dog is one of the best things you can do. It's also one of the most inexpensive ways to maintain your pet's health.

A routine examination will include a physical, weight assessment, and bloodwork. Your veterinarian will note any changes, update any vaccinations that are deemed necessary, and discuss his vaccination protocols with you. Since immune function declines as your dog ages, your veterinarian will decide what vaccines and schedules best suit your dog, considering such factors as his age, breed, lifestyle, and environment.

Rabies vaccinations *must* be kept current. Your dog will also be checked for bordatella risk factors; your veterinarian will ask whether your dog is going to a boarding facility in the near future, and whether he has had any chronic respiratory infections. Your veterinarian will be able to determine your dog's status and risk factors for diseases for which vaccines are available.

Tricks of the Trade

Keeping your dog healthy is the result of a partnership between you and your veterinarian. You can do your part by ensuring that your dog maintains a healthy lifestyle. Diet and exercise are as important for your dog as they are for you. Be observant. Changes in your dog's appetite, movement, or personality warrant a phone call to your veterinarian.

Dogs can become sedentary in their middle years. This is a time when they should be enjoying life, not turning into four-legged couch potatoes. This is when dog sports such as agility, musical freestyle, and flyball (see Chapter 6) can make a real difference in your dog's quality of life, contributing to both physical and mental health. Or you may opt for a daily walk, which is certainly better than no exercise at all. Your dog's fitness is as important as your own, so watch those between-meal snacks and table food. Your dog may beg for it, but you won't be doing him any favors if he becomes obese.

It's a good idea to keep a log of any changes. This need not be a diary—a quick notation on a calendar will suffice. This will allow you to refer to it quickly and find the specific dates when the problem occurred so that you can report it accurately to your veterinarian. If you see a problem and are concerned, call your veterinarian and schedule an appointment to have your dog checked. For example, it could be that your dog is not eating. While he may not have much of an appetite in hot weather, if the lack of appetite continues for more than a day, or if he appears to be ignoring food at any other time, or seems lethargic, it's a good idea to see your veterinarian. It's easier to catch something early than to have to deal with the prolonged treatment of an illness. And if the extra examination shows that there isn't a problem, then you can be assured that your dog is fine. It's better to go to the veterinarian on a false alarm than to wait too long and allow a problem to become worse.

Tricks of the Trade

Obesity is a major cause of health problems in dogs, just as it is in humans. Angell has obesity programs to help get the dog back to his healthiest weight.

You can get nutritional counseling with the staff nutritionist or your primary veterinarian regarding *any* special needs that your dog might have, not just health problems that need dietary management. For example, a dog might be a member of a search-and-rescue team, at work with a police department, or involved in an extremely active dog sport. This working dog's nutritional requirements and feeding schedule will be different from those of the dog with a less active lifestyle. Working dogs should be fed (using a calorically dense, highly digestible diet) four hours before exercise and again after cooldown; alternatively, you could feed just one meal after cooldown. They should be fed small amounts during exercise, since their metabolism will be increased. And diarrhea is common in working dogs. The canine athlete should have either electrolytes in his water or should be drinking an electrolyte solution, just as any athlete would. The liquid in an electrolyte solution is primarily water, but the predominant electrolyte element within the solution is sodium.

If you've adopted an older dog and are not beginning with a puppy, your veterinarian or technician will still show you during an annual checkup how to groom your dog and cut his nails. Your veterinarian is happy to help you learn to take better care of your dog and to answer any questions you may have. Once again, it's important that you have a good rapport and can keep the lines of communication open.

Tricks of the Trade

If your dog's teeth weren't brushed during puppyhood, this is the time when dental problems can begin to show up. Your dog can begin to have a receding gumline, and cavities and periodontal disease can occur. It's never too late to start a dental program to help keep your dog well.

Dental care will be addressed to be certain that the owner is brushing the dog's teeth at home. A dental preventive program will include having the dog's teeth cleaned professionally in order to remove all tartar and to polish the teeth. It may also include x-rays, just as it would for a human, to discover any cavities, gingivitis, or other dental problems below the gumline, and treat them before they become worse. An oral tumor might also be found early during the routine cleaning. A dental procedure will also be necessary if your dog has fractured a tooth. This can happen if he chews on something very hard, like bones.

NUTRITION AND BREEDING

If the dog is involved in a breeding program, he will have special nutritional requirements. Talk with your veterinarian about an appropriate diet for every dog, male and female, involved in a breeding program.

At Angell, the dog is tested for heartworm, and the proper prevention is started once the results of the blood test are known. The dog is checked for other internal and external parasites, and prevention and control of fleas and ticks is discussed.

Training

The annual veterinary visit is also when it will be recommended that you start or continue obedience classes with your dog. It's never too late in your dog's life to teach good behavior. The instructor should be teaching only positive, humane training methods, as we have discussed earlier. The

THYROID DISEASE

Low thyroid (hypothyroid) dogs are chunky and often a little mentally dull, and they may have symmetrical hair loss and a slow heart rate. The dog could have all or none of these signs. It is often recommended that pets be tested for thyroid disease when there are behavioral changes because the thyroid is the primary hormone that regulates metabolism. Behavioral changes can result directly from the metabolic effects.

Hypothyroidism is often a difficult diagnosis to make in dogs. The problem in diagnosis occurs for several reasons:

- False-positive and false-negative test results
- The test can be affected by other medications the dog may be taking
- Breed and age variability in "normal" thyroid hormone levels
- Hypothyroid symptoms tend to be nonspecific

As is the case with most conditions, veterinarians can recognize full-blown disease, but while it's developing they are less able to identify it and intervene. Testing is mandatory before treatment, despite the fact that it is known that some breeds, such as Golden Retrievers and Doberman Pinschers, tend to become hypothyroid as they mature.

trainer should be experienced in working with dogs of all sizes and should not allow classes to become unruly, with the canine version of a bully allowed to dominate. There should be separate classes for puppies and adults, as well as different levels of experience. Feel free to ask for names of people who have taken the classes and contact them to ask about their experiences.

Classes will allow your dog that all-important interaction with members of his own species. It's important the dogs learn to communicate properly with other dogs and enjoy the companionship of their own species.

Don't just rely on class time for training; be sure to practice at home for a few minutes each day, and always end on an upbeat note. Training should be fun for you and your canine companion. Use a happy, positive tone of voice and don't forget to praise your dog for a job well done.

The veterinarian will observe the dog's behavior and question the owner about any behavior problems. This is another time when keeping notes on a calendar, or in a journal, will come in handy. You will have noted any behavioral as well as any physical changes. If there has been a change in behavior, or behavior problems are indicated, a thyroid panel may be suggested to determine whether the problem is an underlying organic (physical) one rather than a behavioral one. Dogs, like people, can act out if they're not feeling well.

If there are behavior problems, a behavior consultation is suggested and can be arranged. Dogs of any size or description can have, or develop,

A PLEASANT PATIENT

While it is your veterinarian's job to examine your pet, it is your responsibility to have a well-mannered dog who can be easily examined. His behavior influences every area of his life, including his visits to the veterinarian. The visits should be pleasant for him, and he should be a polite and cooperative patient. The relationship between your dog and his veterinarian should be one of trust; they should also enjoy being in each other's company.

behavior problems. Of course it's better not to allow problems to begin, and raising the dog with positive training is the best choice. But if your dog has behavior problems—and this can happen for a variety of reasons—it's best to get professional help as soon as possible. Both the dog

THE WELLNESS PROGRAM BLOOD DRIVE

YOUR HEALTHY PET CAN GIVE THE GIFT OF LIFE

Healthy dogs can help less fortunate animals by becoming blood donors at the MSPCA's Angell Memorial Animal Hospital in Boston, Massachusetts. Blood is urgently needed for critically ill and injured animals suffering from disorders like anemia or road accidents and major surgery. Last year more than 150 animals were helped by donated blood.

Donating blood takes only a short time, and both you and your pet will be helping us give much-needed medical care to some of our most critically ill and injured patients.

Donor animals must meet the following requirements:

- Minimum weight of 50 pounds for dogs
- Between one and eight years old
- Current on all vaccinations
- No major medical problems
- Never had a blood transfusion
- Received a physical exam within the past year
- Dobermans and Standard Poodles must be tested for von Willebrand's Disease at owners' expense

As part of the donation procedure, your pet will receive:

- A four-pound bag of food
- A complete physical exam and blood screening
- A heartworm test
- Blood-typing, so if your pet is ever in need of emergency care its blood type will already be on record at Angell
- Eligibility for a free transfusion, should one ever become necessary

From the Animal Wellness Program at Angell Memorial Animal Hospital

and the owner will be happier when any behavior problems or potential behavior problems are resolved. The bond is strengthened when the dog understands that the owner is the leader and he is assured of his place within the family "pack."

Angell has a blood donor program that is discussed with the clients at checkups. Dogs that are ill, have a blood disorder like anemia, are having emergency surgery, or have been in an accident might require a blood transfusion. Your companion can serve as a blood donor, just as you might at a human hospital.

ADULT HANDOUTS

Every client at Angell who has an adult wellness visit with their dog receives a handout about the blood donor program and good nutrition.

Other handouts at the adult visit are not routinely given but are selected on an individual basis. These additional handouts include the following topics:

- Rabies vaccination
- Dental care
- Obesity
- Angell Memorial Animal Hospital's bio and history
- Lyme disease
- Adult obedience
- Parasite control program
- Household toxins, poisonous plants, antifreeze
- Animal Poison Control hotline number and more information related to poisoning
- Anesthesia
- Pet loss and euthanasia
- MSPCA information
- Microchip identification program

A quick tour of the hospital can be requested and scheduled in advance.

Hereditary Diseases

Certain breeds are at risk for certain hereditary diseases, including those of the musculoskeletal system and blood. For example, Doberman Pinschers are at risk for von Willebrand's Disease, Bedlington Terriers are at risk for liver disease, and Basenjis are at risk for Fanconi syndrome. Your veterinarian can screen for these health problems during the annual visit.

At the end of your visit, your pet's health record will be updated by the veterinarian, and Angell clients receive additional handouts.

What We've Learned

Congenital: Existing from the time of birth
Hyperthyroid: High thyroid
Hypothyroid: Low thyroid

10

The Problems of Middle Age

**The middle years are often the most enjoyable
and rewarding time for you and your dog.
It is the time to reap the benefits of your
commitment and hard work through puppyhood.
It is a time when the human–animal bond strengthens
as quality time is spent with your companion.**
— *Douglas Brum, D.V.M.*

Once your dog reaches middle age, health problems can show up at any time. However, between the ages of one and a half and seven years you can probably count on your dog being fairly healthy. Her problems would likely be the result of trauma—if she, for example, got injured or ate something she shouldn't.

You should be habitually alert to changes in your dog's activities and habits. For example, is she drinking less or more than usual? Dogs should not drink more than one ounce per pound of body weight in a twenty-four–hour period, and often they drink significantly less. Watch for weight loss despite a good appetite, weight loss with no appetite, or decreased activity. Be sure she's not getting obese, especially if she has problems with her hip joints, in which case you'll need to decrease the weight on her hips to delay problems. Though your dog is getting older, she should not necessarily be suffering from arthritis.

Issues of training and behavior, such as aggression, can emerge during the middle years, so it's important to continue your dog's training. Canine sports provide a fun way to continue your dog's training throughout her life and give her the exercise she needs to remain fit.

It's always good to be prepared for the unexpected. Veterinary health insurance for your pet can come in handy if your dog faces a chronic or serious medical problem. If you don't have insurance, it's a good idea to have money put aside just in case you are faced with an ongoing medical problem or a medical emergency. Saving for that rainy day is something you can start doing when you first acquire your dog, but it's never too late to open a special bank account for just such an expenditure.

Always have a current photo of your dog handy for identification in case she accidentally escapes from your home, slips away when you're traveling, or needs to be evacuated from your home in an emergency situation such as a flood, fire, or hurricane.

Tricks of the Trade

Environmental enrichment is important. If your yard has different altitudes so that your dog can view her world from different heights, different-sized shrubs, or even toys for toddlers such as little play gyms, it will enhance your dog's quality of life. Make the yard interesting for your dog. And be sure that all fences are secure so that the dog can't jump over it or tunnel under it. Patrol your yard to be sure there's nothing dangerous lying around.

Watch That "Diet"

It's important to keep your dog from running loose so she won't get into garbage, be hit by a car, get into areas with parasite infestations, or acquire mold intoxication. Eating garbage can cause gastrointestinal distress. Gastritis, an inflammation of the stomach, is not unusual in these cases. If your dog remains ill for some time after eating garbage, especially something fatty, she should be evaluated for pancreatitis (see page 169).

Of course, there are many other toxic substances you must keep away from your canine companion. Chocolate is one, as is rat poison. There are two types of rat poison: one can lead to excess vitamin D, which causes kidney failure due to high calcium levels (*hypercalcemia*); the other contains an anticoagulant, which causes bleeding problems. Antifreeze tastes sweet to dogs and is very tempting for them to lick, but a very small amount of it will cause severe and potentially irreversible kidney damage. Many houseplants are also poisonous to dogs. Chapter 11 contains a list of poisonous plants, as well as poison control hotline numbers (page 179).

Introducing Your Adult Dog to a New Dog

If you're planning to bring another dog into your household, you should introduce the newcomer to your dog on neutral territory. Don't simply bring the new dog home, march into the house with him, and expect your dog to accept him. This would be something akin to bringing home a new baby without preparing your child by telling her that a new brother or sister was on the way. Your dog will have the same sort of resentment for the interloper unless introductions are handled properly. It's easier to do it right the first time than to have to remedy problems after the fact.

You can accomplish this in more than one way. You can take your dog along to meet the new dog at his current home, with the permission of the owners. You can also bring home something with the newcomer's scent on it and take something with your dog's scent on it to the new dog's home. Or you can ask about bringing your dog along to the shelter to meet the

new dog on the premises, or just outside in the yard. If you're planning to
bring the new dog directly home, you can have another family member
bring your dog out into the yard and allow the two to meet outdoors
before you bring the newcomer inside. This will give your dog the opportunity to get to know the newcomer and make him welcome in her home.
Give them time. Don't force the issue.

Only good things should happen when the newcomer is in the room—
for example, your dog gets an extra treat. Be sure you give her extra attention so that she doesn't feel that all of the attention is being focused on the
newcomer, or there will be resentment that will be striking in its resem-
blance to sibling rivalry.

Health Issues for Middle-Aged Dogs

Don't miss those annual veterinary appointments, a vital time when your
veterinarian can pick up on the beginning of any potential health problems before they become serious. Physical examinations, blood tests, urine
tests, and such are all important in reaching a diagnosis before a potential
problem has an opportunity to develop.

While some problems might be genetic, others might simply occur,
whether or not your dog is predisposed to them. Hereditary problems will
also occur in mixed-breed dogs. Mixed-breed dogs are not necessarily
healthier than purebred dogs, nor are all purebreds healthier than mixed-
breed dogs.

In the case of the purebred, if the breeder is having her dogs tested for
genetic problems before breeding and doing everything she can to try to
eliminate genetic problems in the bloodlines, then you have a better chance
of acquiring a healthy dog. Ask to see verification of genetic tests from
approved registries such as the Canine Eye Research Foundation (CERF)
and PennHip clearances.

A mixed-breed dog can inherit any genetic health problem that has
occurred in its genetic background. If the dog's background is unknown,
you can try to guess it and ask your veterinarian to look for any possible
sign of genetic defect that might go along with those particular breeds.

It's not uncommon for middle-aged dogs to develop endocrine problems, hypothyroidism being one of the most common. A typical hypothyroid dog will be overweight while at the same time not eating a lot of food, may have symmetrical hair loss, and may be lethargic. It's easily treated, with minimal side effects. (See Chapters 3 and 9 for more information on hypothyroidism.)

Epilepsy

Epilepsy is a chronic medical condition produced by temporary changes in the electrical function of the brain, causing seizures that affect awareness, movement, or sensation. It is one of the most common neurologic conditions that can affect dogs of all breeds. It is more often seen in males than in females, and the age of onset is between one and five years. There are twenty to thirty different types of epilepsy, all suspected to be a result of an unknown brain defect. There may be as many different brain defects as there are epileptic types.

Some seizures can be the result of trauma or disease, but most are thought to be inherited. The dog with a seizure disorder requires a neurological evaluation, as well as a blood screening, including a screening test for lead poisoning.

When a dog is having a seizure, the neurons that transmit impulses to coordinate movement and behavior are out of synch, firing randomly. As a result, the mind and body are not coordinated and are out of control.

There are several types of seizures, including the following.

- *Generalized seizure* involves a sudden loss of consciousness accompanied by twitching; the seizure usually lasts for less than a minute.
- *Grand mal seizure* is a more severe seizure during which the dog may flail uncontrollably.
- *Status epilepticus* is a sustained seizure that can last half an hour or even longer, or it can be a series of smaller seizures. Status epilepticus is an emergency situation that requires rapid treatment— fortunately, it is rare.

- *Cluster seizures* are multiple seizures interspersed with brief periods of consciousness; the cluster seizures can continue to occur for a period of up to twenty-four hours.
- *Petit mal seizures* involve a complete, brief loss of consciousness.
- *Partial seizures* affect only one part of the body.
- *Complex partial seizures* look as if the dog is biting at flies that don't exist, doing a good bit of chewing or licking, twitching on one side of her face, shaking, or even showing aggressive behavior.

Epilepsy is often easier to control in small dogs than large ones, supposedly because the mode of inheritance is different. (This is speculation, of course.) Drugs, such as phenobarbital or potassium bromide, are given on a daily basis at home to prevent seizures. If serious seizures occur, your dog may require hospitalization and rectal or intravenous drugs like Valium to stop the seizures.

Herniated Intervertebral Disc

A herniated disc occurs when the soft gel-like material between vertebrae (spinal bones) ruptures through the covering membrane and pushes against (compresses) the spinal cord. Discs can herniate suddenly as a result of severe trauma in any dog; however, in the breeds most commonly affected (Dachshund, Beagle, Pekingese, Miniature Poodle), they can rupture with normal activity. There is a hereditary predisposition to the breakdown of the membrane that houses the disc, allowing it to rupture easily. Intervertebral disc rupture in the mid- to lower back occurs most commonly between two and eight years of age.

Obesity can either lead to the condition or exacerbate it, which is another good reason to keep your dog at her optimum weight. This condition is quite painful and can result in partial or total paralysis. Treatment includes anti-inflammatory drugs and rest. If the herniated disc results in compression of the spinal cord, surgery to remove the disc should be performed.

Rupture of the Cranial Cruciate Ligament

A rupture of the cranial cruciate ligament (CCL) is the canine equivalent of the rupture of the ACL (anterior cruciate ligament) in humans. It is very common in all breeds of dogs and can occur at any time of life. There is a high incidence in young adult sporting breeds such as the Labrador Retriever, Golden Retriever, and Rottweiler—however, it occurs frequently during the middle years. The injury does not require heavy trauma, but instead is usually associated with normal running and playing. It can begin as an intermittent, mild lameness when the ligament becomes only partially ruptured, or the dog may become acutely lame and unable to bear weight on the affected leg following a sudden and complete rupture. The knee joint becomes unstable following the rupture, and this leads to chronic, irreversible arthritis.

Your veterinarian will be able to make the diagnosis, and she will recommend surgery. Some of the very small dogs can be treated without surgery, but most orthopedic surgeons believe that the best results are achieved with surgery in all cases. Many general practitioners perform the surgery, though you may be referred to a specialist. The prognosis is good, but most patients are left with some arthritis that may need medical management—especially during the later years of life.

Pancreatitis

Pancreatitis is inflammation of the pancreas. Many times it seems to be associated with consuming high-fat food. Vomiting and abdominal discomfort are the main clinical signs. The diagnosis may not be easy to make since it very closely resembles other gastrointestinal diseases and definitive tests are not available. Your veterinarian will likely do blood enzyme tests, amylase and lipase tests, and an ultrasound.

Treatment of pancreatitis begins with the withholding of food. Since your dog will likely not feel like eating, this is not usually a problem. The point is to rest the enzyme-producing cells in the pancreas. Dogs with severe pancreatitis need to be hospitalized, possibly for two weeks (or longer), and many times require critical care treatment. In the future, watching her diet carefully will be more important than ever.

Diabetes Mellitus

Diabetes mellitus is a metabolic disorder that is characterized by insulin deficiency. It usually affects dogs that are middle-aged or older, and it may be seen in any breed. Similar to juvenile-onset diabetes in humans, canine diabetes is also treated with insulin. Diet plays an important part in the management of this disease. There is thought to be a genetic predisposition to the disease.

If a dog is drinking excessively and losing weight, diabetes should be suspected. A physical examination by your veterinarian and blood glucose (sugar) test will confirm the diagnosis so that treatment can begin as soon as possible. The dog with diabetes will require a consistent diet and carefully balanced insulin injections on a regular schedule. She should be fed two low-fat, low-sugar meals per day. Moderate- to high-fiber diets may decrease the amount of insulin needed. Regular exercise should also be part of the routine for your dog. Your veterinarian will show you how to monitor your dog's glucose level before giving insulin injections. This may require urine testing.

Cushing's Disease

Otherwise known as *hyperadrenocorticism*, Cushing's disease is caused when excessive cortisol, a natural steroid hormone, is produced by the adrenal gland. The symptoms, which include thirst, hair loss, increased urination, panting, and weakness, can appear if the dog is taking steroids and has too much in her system—but in that case, the symptoms will disappear when you stop using the steroids (which can be found in some ointments, creams, and such). These signs, however, are more commonly caused by oral steroids.

Cushing's disease is considered one of the most common endocrine disorders in dogs. The breeds in which it's seen most often are Poodles, Dachshunds, Boxers, Beagles, and Boston Terriers. It is most often caused by a lesion in the pituitary gland at the base of the brain. In far fewer cases, one of the adrenal glands has a tumor that excretes cortisol independently. The tumors can be removed surgically, though the malignant tumor is nearly always fatal. Medication that suppresses the secretion of cortisol must be given in appropriate doses. Cushing's disease can be a complex condition to treat, but it can be managed successfully and needs to be monitored carefully.

Chronic Valvular Heart Disease

Gradually developing abnormalities on the heart valves can lead to serious heart function problems over a long period of time. Middle age may be the time when the veterinarian can first detect a heart murmur, the tip-off that the heart isn't functioning correctly. Treatment would not necessarily begin at this time, but it's likely that your veterinarian will want to monitor your dog's heart function. Later, you and your veterinarian can put into place a treatment management plan.

Urinary Stones

Stones form when the dog's urine is too concentrated with minerals to maintain the properties of a fluid. The most common types of stones are struvite and calcium oxylate.

Struvites are seen mainly in young female dogs; they result from a urinary tract infection. Diet can help minimize the recurrence of struvite stones, but it's also important that they be medically treated. A special diet can help avoid surgery, and antibiotics are given while the stones are being dissolved. The stones trap bacteria in them, hence the need for antibiotics. Follow-up urine cultures can help to prevent more struvite stones.

Calcium oxylate stones are seen more frequently in some breeds than others. Shih Tzu, Yorkshire Terriers, and Lhasa Apsos can form them at a young age. These stones are rarely found in large dogs. No one really knows why calcium oxylate stones form, although there seem to be dietary associations. Feeding table scraps and excessive treats seem to coincide with the formation of these stones. Calcium oxylate stones must be physically removed from the dog through either surgery or the more expensive lithotrypsy, which uses a shock wave to break up the stones; the tiny pieces are voided in the dog's urine. If the stone is small enough to pass through the urethra, another nonsurgical method of removing them, voiding urohydropropulsion, can be used. In that procedure the urologist must distend the bladder and position the dog so her spine is vertical. The stones then drop into the urethral opening and the urologist can then express the bladder, which voids urine and stones simultaneously.

Once the stones are gone, the dog can be fed a special diet to help prevent recurrence. The best way to avoid stone formation is to be sure your dog is drinking enough water. If you can't get your dog to drink more, then you can consider switching to a canned food because the canned diets are usually about 70 percent water.

Urinary Tract Infections

Urinary tract infections are common in dogs, and in most cases are easily treated. The classic signs include increased frequency of urination, urinating in the house, a strong odor to the urine, blood in the urine (pink or red), and/or difficulty (straining) when urinating. If you observe any of these signs, you should have your dog examined because these signs can also be associated with more serious problems, such as cancers of the urinary tract. Your veterinarian will be able to make a diagnosis after performing an exam and obtaining data from urinalysis, blood tests, and possibly x-rays.

What We've Learned

Glucose: Commonly referred to as sugar in diabetic animals or humans

Petit mal: A complete, brief loss of consciousness

Status epilepticus: A long, continuous seizure that can last half an hour or more, or a series of smaller seizures

11

Emergencies and First Aid

It is human nature to procrastinate when preparing
for emergencies. Read this chapter well and take the
preparation steps indicated. It is comforting to know
you are prepared for the worst, and it is so difficult to
react logically and properly if you are not prepared
when the pet you love is seriously ill or injured.

—Peter Theran, V.M.D.,
Diplomate, A.C.V.I.M.

It would be wonderful if life ran smoothly, if everything went according to plan, and we never had to deal with emergencies. But emergencies do happen. Knowing this, we should be prepared to face them and deal with them when they occur. Be certain that your veterinarian has emergency coverage or that there is an emergency veterinary clinic nearby.

What's an Emergency?

Take your dog to your veterinarian immediately if any of the following occurs.

- Trauma (hit by car, long fall, penetrating wounds), even if the animal looks OK at the time
- Poisoning (toxicity) or potential toxicity
- Large open wounds to any part of the body
- Large-breed dog with unproductive retching (may have gastric dilatation-volvulus—see Chapter 5)
- Bleeding or fractures
- Electric shock
- Eye injury
- Difficult labor
- Severe vomiting and diarrhea, particularly if bloody or associated with weakness
- Poorly responsive to the owner (or unconscious) or unable to move around
- Acute onset of paralysis (sudden inability to walk)
- Inability to urinate
- A diabetic dog who is vomiting or lethargic, and not eating
- Difficulty breathing
- Fire or smoke inhalation, even if the dog appears OK at the time
- If the dog has *known* kidney failure, heart disease (and is on medications), bleeding disorder anemia, or Addison's disease, and is suddenly not doing well at home
- A dog with white/pale gums or rapid heart rate who is weak and behaving abnormally
- A dog who has received bite wounds, even if the dog looks OK at the time
- Fracture with the bone exposed
- Possible ingestion of a foreign body (for example, a toy, needle, pin, or tinsel), with profuse vomiting and sick appearance

Call the veterinary hospital first, if there's time, or have someone call for you, to alert them that you are on your way in with an emergency. Briefly describe the emergency so the staff can be prepared for your arrival. If there's no time, and no one available to call, just get in your car and drive to the hospital immediately.

Some common medical emergencies warrant further discussion.

Heatstroke

Heatstroke usually occurs during hot months, especially in dogs that are confined in poorly ventilated areas such as cars. Even cracking open your car windows may not be enough, because cars quickly overheat. Your dog is safer being left at home in an air-conditioned environment if he is not welcome inside stores where you are running errands.

Hot weather is especially difficult for dogs that are old and overweight, as well as those that are brachycephalic or have heart or lung disease. Dogs with black coats also seem to suffer more in hot weather.

Tricks of the Trade

When walking your dog on very hot days, try to avoid the hottest part of the day—from 11 to 2 in the afternoon. And always feel the pavement with your hand. If it's too hot for your bare hand, it's too hot for the pads of your dog's feet.

Heatstroke is dangerous because it can lead to tissue damage, bleeding inside the dog's head (*intracranial hemorrhage*), nerve cell death, death of other cells in the body, and liver and kidney damage. Symptoms of heatstroke include rapid breathing, rapid heart rate, depression, diarrhea, vomiting, dehydration, seizures, and collapse. Death usually follows the development of such signs.

Your best course of action is to give the dog a cold bath, wrap him in a cold wet towel, and transport him to the nearest veterinarian as quickly as possible. If he will drink, oral fluids should be encouraged. Once he's at the clinic, IV fluids will be given to prevent shock. He will be bathed in cold water or rubbing alcohol and may be placed in front of a fan. Cooling will stop and the dog will be dried once his temperature has dropped. The veterinarian will continue to check the dog's temperature hourly and closely monitor for further complications.

Burns

Dogs can receive burns in a number of ways. Most burns are caused by heat (blow dryers, heating pads, contact with fire or boiling liquids). Here are some of the more common ways in which dogs can receive burns:

- Contact with a chemical agent
- Being dragged over pavement
- Chewing on an electrical cord (which can happen with puppies that aren't carefully supervised—it's wise to tape cords to the wall so curious pups can't get into trouble)

How quickly the burn will heal depends on its severity. The prognosis for a given patient depends on the cause of the burn and percentage of the body that is involved. A severe burn can cause shock, as well as metabolic, kidney, and respiratory disorders. Life-threatening infections can occur.

Minor burns are usually treated with a topical agent such as lidocaine. If severe burns are discovered within two hours, and if the dog is cooperative, ice-water packs can be applied to reduce pain and swelling. In the case of a chemical burn it's important to remove any of the substance still on the skin. Severe burns require appropriate wound management and, in some cases, skin grafts.

Frostbite

Those who live in a cold climate are accustomed to frostbite warnings. But they might not realize that their dogs can also be affected if they are exposed to freezing temperatures over a period of time. Skin lesions resulting from frostbite will appear at the tips of the ears or the tip of the tail, or on the scrotum. Frostbitten skin will be pale and cool to the touch. As with humans, the skin should be thawed very gently using warm water. After thawing, the changes in the skin may range from redness and scaling in mild cases to necrosis (morphological changes that indicate the death of cells) and sloughing in severe cases.

Frostbite is easily prevented with common sense. Dogs that live in cold climates and are bred for outdoor activities, such as the Alaskan Malamute and Siberian Husky, will find the cold less problematic. Small dogs, however, lose body heat more rapidly than larger dogs, as do those with very short coats and little fat, such as the Greyhound. If your dog is not adjusted to the climate, or his coat is short, he should not be outdoors for a long period of time and will benefit from a sweater or coat.

Poisoning

A dog can be poisoned in any number of ways, often by seemingly inoffensive products and substances lying around the house. So it's important to pet-proof your home to protect your dog, just as you would childproof it to protect your children.

Store household products where your pet can't reach them. Many people keep these in a cabinet under the kitchen sink, thinking the dog can't open the cabinet doors. But intelligent dogs have figured out how to do this time and again, so it's best to buy child-safe locks for that cabinet. If your pet ingests one of these toxic products, it can lead to death.

In the same way, keep all human and canine medicine out of the reach of curious pets. If there's an elderly person at home who is taking

Tricks of the Trade

If you live in a climate where snow and ice are a factor, be sure to wash the pads of your dog's feet after a walk. If the roadways or any pavement surfaces have been treated with an ice melter, you need to wash that off before your dog licks his paws and ingests any of the potentially poisonous substance.

medication, be sure that none of it falls to the floor. It's all too easy for someone whose hands may shake to drop pills, and a dog can reach that medication quite quickly. (This is another time when teaching commands such as "Leave it!" or "Look at me!" can come in handy.)

The symptoms of chemical poisoning include vomiting, difficulty breathing, unusual drooling, burns in or around the mouth, unusual behavior, convulsions, or unconsciousness.

POISONOUS PLANTS

Here are some of the plants poisonous to dogs that are commonly found in homes or in the garden.

Aloe vera	Cyclamen	Narcissus
Amaryllis	Daffodil	Oleander
Apple seeds	Dieffenbachia	Onions
Apricot pits	Easter lily	Rhododendron
Azalea	English ivy	Sweetheart ivy
Bird of paradise	Geranium	Tomato plant
Calla lily	Kalanchoe	Yew
Clematis	Mistletoe	

Incorrectly using an insecticide on a dog, or using too much of the product, can also lead to poisoning. Many houseplants can also be poisonous to your pet (see the list on the previous page). Either keep them out of the pet's reach or don't keep them in your home at all.

If you suspect that your dog has ingested a toxic substance or poisonous plant, you should call an emergency pet poison hotline (see below) or your veterinarian immediately. Try to give precise information such as the exact substance, the amount ingested, the time of ingestion, and the dog's present condition.

It's a good idea to have hydrogen peroxide or syrup of ipecac on hand in case of poisoning. The emergency pet poison hotline will tell you how much hydrogen peroxide or ipecac you should give to your dog to help eliminate what is in his stomach before you rush him to your veterinarian.

POISON CONTROL HOTLINES

Along with your veterinarian's phone number, you should have a poison control hotline number next to your telephone. The American Society for the Prevention of Cruelty to Animals (ASPCA) has a national twenty-four–hour poison control hotline staffed by veterinarians: (888) 426-4435. Kansas State University's College of Veterinary Medicine offers another poison control hotline staffed by veterinarians twenty-four hours a day. The hotline's local number is (785) 532-5679; the national toll-free number is (800) 222-1222. There may be a charge for these services, but it is, obviously, worth every penny that it may cost. The College of Veterinary Medicine at the University of Illinois at Urbana-Champaign has a center that is staffed around the clock by veterinary professionals; call (800) 548-2423. If you know what your dog consumed, be prepared to tell the hotline operator what it was and how much the dog seems to have ingested. Take the box or bottle to the phone with you, if possible. In cases of emergency, call one of these hotlines first and then get in touch with your veterinarian for treatment.

Always get the advice of a veterinarian before administering either hydrogen peroxide or syrup of ipecac. Also, keep in mind that some of the things a dog can ingest can be acidic, alkaline, or might contain petroleum, in which case you should *not* induce vomiting.

Electric Shock

If your dog or puppy bites into an electric cord, get him to a veterinarian immediately. Electric shock is believed to be responsible for a form of acute heart failure; it may also cause fluid buildup in the lungs, and there are indications that the electrical current may cause damage to pulmonary capillaries. If there is a burn, an oral examination will show a white, seared area across the tongue or lips.

Even though your dog may appear normal after the injury, your veterinarian will want to watch him for at least two or three hours after the injury. Chest x-rays will likely be taken, and oxygen may be administered.

Vehicle-Related Accidents

Despite owners' best efforts to keep dogs safe, they sometimes do get loose, and it takes only a moment for one to run into the street and be hit by a vehicle. Even if it's your own dog who has been hit and injured, you cannot rule out the possibility of being bitten by the hurting and frightened animal. Your dog doesn't mean to bite you, but if he's in a significant amount of pain he'll clamp down.

Approach him with a calm demeanor so as not to upset him any further. Talk calmly and reassuringly to him as you fashion a muzzle out of gauze so that he cannot bite you. Feel his body to determine whether there are any broken bones. Then get him to a veterinarian as quickly as possible. If he's a large dog, you'll need help moving him to a flat board and putting him, on that board, into your car for transport. Keep him as still as possible to prevent further injury. Time is of the essence—you don't know what sort of internal injuries may have occurred.

First Aid

When an emergency situation arises, you may be able to do certain things to assist your dog before you can get him to the veterinarian. Following are some basic first aid tips that dog owners should know.

First Aid Kit

You should have a first aid kit accessible at all times. It's easy to make one using a fishing tacklebox, small toolbox, or any other latched box that has

URGENT APPOINTMENT GUIDELINES

Some nonemergency situations are nevertheless serious enough that you cannot wait a few days for a regular veterinary appointment. In such cases you should make an *urgent appointment*. Urgent situations include the following.

- A referral that needs an elective *endoscopy* (examination of the organs that can be seen through an *endoscope*, a special instrument that's inserted through the mouth for this purpose) but cannot wait for a regular appointment because the dog isn't stable enough
- A medicine/cardiology/neurology/oncology referral that needs a medical workup but cannot wait for a regular appointment because the dog isn't stable enough
- A dog that is vomiting and has diarrhea but is still relatively active and alert
- A dog with a fracture that a referring veterinarian is sending to a major institution or specialty hospital for surgery
- An apparently healthy dog with unexplained severe lameness
- A dog with ear infections or hot spots
- Any dog not eating and/or losing weight—if the dog appears weak, this will require an urgent appointment; if the dog is healthy, he can wait for a regular appointment

Tricks of the Trade

Always have your first aid kit in a handy place so you don't have to go searching for it. You'll be stressed enough if there's an emergency without adding to the pressure by frantically trying to locate the supplies you need.

compartments so you can put things in places where they're easily located when you need them.

If you do a lot of traveling with your dog, you might consider having two: one that stays at home in an easily accessible place, and another that's in the car. Even if you travel infrequently, you should always take your dog's first aid kit with you. Don't forget to check the kit periodically to be certain that all dated items are current and that all of the items are in the box. And be sure to keep an extra blanket in your car.

Write your name, address, and telephone number on the outside of the box in case you lose it. Include your veterinarian's telephone number, as well as the telephone number of a local veterinary emergency facility and an animal poison control center. If you're traveling, try to secure the name and phone number of a trusted veterinarian before you leave. Ask your veterinarian for a referral, or ask a friend who lives in the area.

Before you travel it's a good idea to have separate information sheets for each pet. Include a photo of each pet with the name, age, breed, sex, identification (owner contact information, microchipping information), and any health problems. This can help if your pet is lost or if someone unfamiliar with your pet is needed to care for him.

A well-stocked first aid kit for dogs includes the following.

- Roll cotton
- Cotton balls
- Gauze pads
- Gauze tape
- Hydrogen peroxide (check the expiration date)

- Hydrocortisone ointment
- Antibiotic ointment
- Scissors
- Eyewash
- Silver nitrate
- Tweezers
- Thermometer (both oral and rectal thermometers can be used rectally)
- Oral syringes
- Balanced electrolyte fluid
- Baby food (meat flavors work best)
- Large towel
- Exam gloves
- 1-inch white tape (in addition to gauze tape)
- Rolls of elastic wrap
- Emergency icepack
- Magnifying glass
- Flashlight and/or penlight
- Aspirin (know the correct dose, and ensure that your dog can tolerate it)

Taking Your Dog's Temperature

One of the first duties of first aid you should learn is how to take your dog's temperature. Your veterinarian can demonstrate the best method. Put some petroleum jelly on the tip of the thermometer, lift your dog's tail, and place the thermometer, by gently rotating it, into the rectum. It should be inserted about one or two inches, less for a tiny dog. In about a minute or two you should have an accurate reading. Remember to talk quietly to your dog and remain calm so you won't cause him to become anxious.

Your dog's temperature should be between 99.5 and 102.5 degrees Fahrenheit. Anything above 103 degrees Fahrenheit is considered a fever (unless the dog is excited). You can also use an ototympanic thermometer, which is placed into the dog's ear, to get a quick and accurate reading. There are also temperature strips that can be placed on the dog's skin. These will give you a quick reading, but possibly a slightly less accurate one.

What to Do in an Emergency

The first thing to do in an emergency is to create a temporary muzzle for your dog. Pain can cause even the most loving and trusting dog to bite. If he has a broken limb, try to keep it stable by using a board or even the handle from a broom. A ruler can be used to stabilize the leg of a small dog. Create a makeshift stretcher from an ironing board or an old door if one is available, so that you can carry the dog to the car. Do not carry the dog in your arms. He must be placed on something flat and stable— moving him too much will cause him more pain and can do more damage. Have someone call the veterinary hospital, if possible, to let the staff there know you are on the way with an emergency so they can be prepared when you arrive.

What We've Learned

Necrosis: Death of cells or of the body
Toxicity: Poisoning

12

Fighting Against Cancer

The diagnosis of cancer is no longer an
automatic death sentence. Recent medical
advances and treatment options may offer
a far better outcome than could have been
expected in previous years. Being well educated
is an owner's important first step in making
the best decision for one's pet.

—Douglas Brum, D.V.M.

Cancer is a word that strikes fear in the hearts of those who hear it. Unfortunately, it's affecting pets as much as it's affecting people. In fact, it has been called the number-one disease killer of dogs. We certainly hear more about cancer today than in years past, but it's hard to say whether that's because there's more cancer or because it's easier to diagnose and treat it. Twenty-five years ago, if a veterinarian operated on a dog and found cancer, he would close the incision and the dog would either go home to live out however many days she had left or be humanely euthanized. Today there are treatment options that can give your dog some additional quality time.

There are many forms of cancer, and the disease can strike any dog at any time. While many effective treatments are available, there is no guarantee of complete cure at this time, despite ongoing research into the disease.

Cancer Prevention

Simply spaying or neutering your dog has cancer prevention benefits. Males that are neutered will not get testicular cancer, and females spayed before the first heat have a drastically reduced risk of mammary cancer.

The best prevention is watchfulness. While some tumors may be benign (not cancerous), it's important to have anything unusual checked by your veterinarian as soon as possible. This is another reason why regular groom-

CANCER WARNING SIGNS

Here's a checklist of the warning signs of cancer. These symptoms are also seen in lots of other diseases. If your dog is showing some of these signs, don't panic. The dog probably does not have cancer. These are just general symptoms. Contact your veterinarian if your dog is exhibiting any of these symptoms.

- Abnormal swellings that continue to grow
- Sores or ulcers that do not heal in two weeks
- Weight loss, loss of appetite, loss of energy
- A pale color of the mucous membranes
- Bad breath, loose teeth, offensive odor, chronic sneezing, or runny eyes
- Difficulty eating or swallowing; salivation; vomiting
- Difficulty breathing, urinating, or defecating
- Trouble walking; hesitation to exercise
- Severe pain and acute lameness without history of trauma
- Bleeding or discharge from any body opening
- Increased water intake or urine output

ing is such a good idea—it will give you the opportunity to discover anything unusual on the skin. In the same way, brushing the dog's teeth regularly will allow you to discover any oral tumors. It's best, of course, to discover the problem early and begin treatment as soon as possible.

Diagnosing Cancer

The veterinarian may take a biopsy of the tumor surgically and examine it under the microscope to determine whether it's malignant (cancerous) or benign (noncancerous). Other means of cancer detection include *aspiration biopsy*, in which the veterinarian uses a needle with a syringe to plunge into the tumor and remove (*aspirate*) some cells to be viewed under a microscope. This examination process is called *cytology* and requires special training. X-rays also help in the diagnosis of cancer, sometimes before the onset of signs, as it does for women who have mammograms. Ultrasound, tomography (CT scan), magnetic resonance imaging (MRI), and nuclear scintigraphy (scans) are also used to detect and stage (determine the extent of) cancer.

Treating Cancer

There are three main methods of treating cancer: surgery, chemotherapy, and radiation. The dog's general physical condition, age, and type of cancer will be taken into consideration when deciding the best treatment options.

Surgery

Cancerous tumors are composed of cells that multiply and destroy the surrounding normal tissue. Malignant cells can spread through the body by way of either the bloodstream or the lymphatic vessels; such cancers are said to *metastasize*. Benign tumors don't spread—however, depending on their size and location, they can require removal.

Surgery is particularly effective for self-contained, or *encapsulated*, tumors. Whenever possible, the surgeon removes a wide margin of normal tissue around the tumor in order to ensure the complete removal of abnormal tissue. Of course, the surgeon cannot see every cell, so the margins of the removed tissue are examined under a microscope by a pathologist to check for the presence of cancer cells.

Chemotherapy

Chemotherapy is the use of toxic agents (chemicals) to destroy cancerous cells. It's used to treat tumors that are likely to metastasize. Chemotherapy may be used in combination with surgery and/or radiation therapy. People often wonder whether their dog will suffer the same chemotherapy side effects that often occur in humans, such as hair loss and nausea. Veterinary oncologists usually select drug protocols that do not cause painful side effects.

At Angell Memorial Animal Hospital, severe chemotherapy side effects are usually not seen. If an animal experiences severe side effects, the vet-

TREATMENT OF SIDE EFFECTS

Here are some things you can do if your dog experiences any of the following side effects of chemotherapy.

Nausea
- Withhold food temporarily. Offer ice cubes every few hours.
- Feed small, frequent meals rather than one large meal.

Not Drinking Fluids
- Offer chicken or beef broth.
- Call the clinic if the condition persists longer than twenty-four hours.

erinarians at Angell will either lower the next dose of that drug, skip that drug entirely, or change to a different drug. Most of Angell's patients experience only mild side effects, such as temporary nausea, lethargy, reduced appetite, and mild diarrhea for a few days after treatment. If the dog is treated with drugs known to cause side effects, the client will be given the information in the sidebar at the bottom of these pages.

Before the next visit, withhold food the morning of the visit and call one week in advance to schedule an appointment. It is recommended that you wait two months after your animal receives chemotherapy to resume vaccinations.

Radiation

The use of radiation allows for the targeting of specific areas, as a radioactive beam is sent directly to the cancerous cells to destroy them. Radiation therapy requires general anesthesia, and treatments are usually given daily for about three weeks. Many animals are treated as outpatients, coming into the office and staying for an hour (which includes treatment, anesthesia, and

Vomiting
- Withhold food for twelve hours.
- Offer small, bland meals, such as chicken or veal baby food. Gradually introduce normal diet.
- Call the clinic if the condition persists longer than twenty-four hours.

Diarrhea
- Feed bland food, such as chicken or veal baby food, boiled chicken, or lamb mixed with cooked rice.
- Call the clinic if the condition persists.

Increased Thirst or Urination
- Call the clinic if this persists more than four to five days.

recovery). Radiation therapy is usually well tolerated. Side effects are variable and depend on the area of the body that's being irradiated.

Pain Management

It is important, of course, to maintain the canine cancer patient's quality of life. Pain management is a vital part of this undertaking, and pain-control medication is available. The pain experienced will depend on the type of cancer the dog has. If a brain tumor can cause behavioral changes, then why can't it cause a headache? By the same token, inflammations and infections can also be painful to an animal, as can tumors that put pressure on nerves or invade organs. Pain control is a humane treatment option for animals being treated for cancer. Cancer patients receive careful monitoring to ensure that their needs are met. Your veterinarian or veterinary oncologist will determine the best pain-relief medication and protocol for your dog depending on her circumstances.

Diet and Cancer

It has been speculated that diet and cancer are linked. Dr. Greg Ogilvie at Colorado State University has been a principal investigator of this theory, and his research has helped to develop a commercial therapeutic diet. Clinical studies showed that the diet helped keep dogs treated for lymphoma in remission for an additional 100 days, as compared to the dogs in the study who were fed a common diet. Veterinary nutritionists have undertaken the task of helping formulate a homemade diet to help dogs undergoing cancer treatment to maintain their weight. While some pet owners are looking to nutraceuticals to help their pets with cancer, there is no way for the pet owner to truly know which nutraceuticals will help and which are "snake oil." It is best to talk with your veterinarian, veterinary oncologist, or a veterinary nutritionist about a specific diet if your dog has cancer.

Types of Cancer

There are several types of cancer that can occur in animals, just as in humans. Some breeds of dogs are more prone to some types of cancers than others. Here are some of the more common ones.

Lymphoma

One of the most common cancers in dogs is lymphoma—cancer of the lymphocytes, which are found in the bone marrow, blood, lymph nodes, and even in some abdominal organs. Lymphoma can appear in all of these areas. The more organ systems involved, the more serious the cancer.

The average dog with lymphoma is between six and nine years of age, although dogs of any age can be affected. Certain breeds (Boxer, German Shepherd, Golden Retriever, Scottish Terrier, West Highland White Terrier, and Pointer) may be more likely to develop this type of cancer. Males and females are equally at risk. In most cases, the cause of lymphoma cannot be determined.

Symptoms of lymphoma vary greatly. Some dogs may feel quite ill. Other dogs may feel fine, but the owner has noticed that unusual lumps (enlarged lymph nodes) have suddenly appeared. Enlarged lymph nodes are the most common presentation of lymphoma in dogs. Commonly affected lymph nodes include the ones located under the jaw, in front of the shoulders, in the groin, in the "armpits," and behind the knees. These types of lymphoma are usually diagnosed by an aspirate or biopsy of the enlarged lymph node. Other types of lymphoma are diagnosed by examining the blood, bone marrow, or other tissue samples. Once lymphoma has been diagnosed, your veterinarian may send you to a referral hospital for consultation with a veterinary oncologist.

Lymphoma is usually treated with chemotherapy. Depending on the type and extent of disease, some dogs might go into remission for a year. Many dogs with lymphoma will feel quite good while on chemotherapy. A good quality life is a primary goal of treatment.

While protocols may vary from one veterinarian to another, discuss treatment carefully with your veterinarian. The goal is the longest possible survival with the greatest possible quality of life.

Bone Cancer

Osteosarcoma is a fairly common bone cancer in the Giant breeds (Great Dane and St. Bernard, for example) and larger dogs (such as the German Shepherd, Rottweiler, and Golden Retriever). Dogs with bone cancer often exhibit lameness and swelling, and sometimes there has been trauma to the area first. The most common treatment is amputation of the affected leg; however, in very specific cases, veterinarians at Angell have been performing limb-sparing surgery for many years. In this surgery a bone graft from a deceased dog is donated and replaces the diseased portion of bone, thus allowing the dog to retain her leg. It should be noted, however, that dogs do very well with three legs instead of four and quickly adjust after amputation.

Mast Cell Cancer

Mast cell tumors are extremely common in dogs. They are seen most often in Boxers, Boston Terriers, Labrador Retrievers, Golden Retrievers, Weimaraners, Bulldogs, and Shar-Pei. Mast cell tumors appear on the outer surface of the skin and are surgically removed. The mass may grow quickly with rapid change of color, but since it's confined to the skin there's usually no systemic illness symptom. Animals are generally asymptomatic, but some dogs may be ill if the tumor is extensive. Because mast cell tumors are so common, they are the second most fatal tumor in dogs.

A fine needle aspiration is usually enough to diagnose a mast cell tumor. Your veterinarian will perform several tests to determine the stage of the tumor. The tests will include a complete blood count, a serum chemistry profile, urinalysis, x-rays, and perhaps an abdominal ultrasound. Treatment will depend on the diagnosis of the stage as well as the location of the tumor. Depending on the malignancy, the surgical procedure may be enough—but if the tumors begin to spread, then radiation or chemotherapy may be indicated.

Malignant Melanoma

This is the most common oral tumor found in dogs. Cocker Spaniels, German Shepherds, Chows, and dogs with heavily pigmented mucous membranes are said to be predisposed to this condition, with males more frequently affected than females. Oral bleeding and bad breath are among the most common signs of malignant melanoma, as is a reluctance to chew. The size of the tumor will help determine the prognosis—dogs with smaller tumors have a better survival rate. The cancer can move to the lungs. Diagnosis is made with the help of radiography and biopsy. Malignant melanomas are treated with surgical removal, but the success varies depending on the location of the tumor. In advanced cases, surgery, radiation, and chemotherapy may be necessary, but malignant melanomas of the mouth and feet are difficult to control.

Squamous Cell Carcinoma

The second most common oral malignancy in dogs is squamous cell carcinoma. It usually begins with the lining of the gums, which may become red, ulcerated, and thickened. Large-breed dogs are predisposed to this condition, and prognosis will depend on the location of the tumor. Those located toward the nose have a better prognosis than those at the base of the tongue or in the tonsils, as they are difficult to remove, tend to metastasize, and become the most aggressive. They can be removed surgically, or the veterinarian may choose to use radiation.

Fibrosarcoma

The third most common oral malignancy in dogs, fibrosarcoma, occurs in no particularly common site. It occasionally invades the muscle and bone and destroys local tissue. It's invasive but seldom metastasizes. Surgery is usually the treatment of choice.

Hemangiosarcoma

Hemangiosarcoma is an extremely aggressive cancer of blood vessels, usually in the spleen. It is seen most commonly in German Shepherds and Golden Retrievers. Many times these tumors grow rapidly and may rupture and bleed. This causes a rapid loss of blood into the abdomen, and anemia and shock may ensue. The spleen is generally removed to diagnose and treat the condition. Even with surgery, the cancer has usually spread and the prognosis is poor for more than a few months. Chemotherapy after surgery may improve the survival time, but ultimately this is often a fatal cancer.

Cancer and its treatment options should always be thoroughly discussed with your veterinarian. Some cancers are treatable with a good prognosis; some can be controlled for long periods while your dog maintains a good quality of life; and some cannot be treated. Understanding this will help you make the best possible choices for your dog.

What We've Learned

Aspiration and cytology: The sampling of a mass using a needle, then analyzing the retrieved cells microscopically

Benign: Not cancerous

Biopsy: Removing a core or wedge of tissue for a more accurate microscopic analysis

Encapsulated: Enclosed, self-contained

Malignant: Cancerous

PART III

The Senior Canine

13

Aging Gracefully

You and your pet know each other well now.
Age brings the loss of some capabilities.
Adjust to help where you can, and enjoy
those things that work well for both of you.
— *Peter Theran, V.M.D.,*
Diplomate, A.C.V.I.M.

The years seem to fly by as the bond between you and your dog strengthens. You seem to understand each other almost intuitively now. It probably seems like only yesterday that you brought your dog home, but time is passing . . . and that graying muzzle tells you that the clock is ticking.

Geriatric Exams

As with people, dogs' body parts start to wear out, and function diminishes with age. It's a good idea at this stage to schedule two checkups per year to ensure that your dog stays healthy and that any changes can be discovered and treated early. A typical geriatric visit protocol is described in the "Geriatric Wellness" handout given to Angell clients (page 199). The table below offers general guidelines for the frequency of your senior dog's geriatric visits based on his size and age.

As always, you will be asked to bring a small stool sample. You will also be asked to fast your dog (not feed him) for twelve hours before the visit, if possible. In some cases it may not be possible, and your veterinarian will advise you of that based on your dog's condition. Water should never be withheld, so do be certain that fresh water is available to him during this time. Angell clients are asked not to allow their dog to urinate before the examination, if possible, so that a urine sample can be obtained. They also are asked to arrive five to ten minutes early to fill out a geriatric history form (page 200).

Ideally, a blood pressure reading is taken before the examination, but if the dog is overly excited, stressed, or difficult to handle, this won't be possible. The veterinarian will review the dog's history with the owner before performing a complete physical examination. Additional diagnostic tests may be done based on the history and the results of the physical examination. The technician and the veterinarian will also review internal and external parasite programs with the owner, and preventive measures will be continued. The handout on page 202 shows the various factors Angell veterinarians take into consideration at geriatric appointments.

As your dog attains senior status, he should have bloodwork done to establish his normal levels of various body functions, especially kidney

Recommended Schedule for Geriatric Appointments

Size	Yearly Geriatric Exam	Exam Every Six Months
Small (less than 20 lb)	Ages 11–13	Age 14 or older
Medium (21–50 lb)	Ages 10–11	Age 12 or older
Large (51–90 lb)	Ages 6–8	Age 8 or older
Giant (more than 90 lb)	Ages 6–8	Age 8 or older

GERIATRIC WELLNESS

At Angell Memorial Animal Hospital, we place a strong emphasis on preventive medicine. In many animals, it is easier to prevent problems from occurring, or find problems before they become symptomatic, than it is to treat an existing disease. For older animals, this may be even more significant, requiring a strong commitment from you and your veterinarian. The Geriatric Wellness Program was established to better serve clients with older pets.

A geriatric appointment begins before you and your pet arrive at the hospital. A wellness technician will speak with you over the phone, detailing what to expect at your visit and advising you how to prepare for it. A geriatric history sheet will be sent to your home. We ask you to closely observe your pet, and make note of habits that may have long become familiar to you. These observations can provide your veterinarian with important information that might otherwise be overlooked.

The time scheduled for a geriatric exam is forty minutes. Extra time is included for a complete physical exam, sample collection (for blood tests and urinalysis), and any diagnostics the veterinarian feels appropriate based on the physical findings. Specific tests are designed to detect abnormal or deteriorating function of vital organs, such as the liver, kidneys, or pancreas. Your pet's exam and diagnostic results will be thoroughly explained to you by your veterinarian. Additionally, the results will be forwarded to you on a completed geriatric wellness assessment sheet. Questions are welcomed, and you will be educated on how to continue monitoring the health of your geriatric pet at home.

Within a week, the nutritionist on staff will contact you regarding any dietary recommendations based on the exam. Our dental office will contact you if dental prophylaxis or home dental care is advised. Finally, the wellness technician will follow up on any questions you have and is always available, should more arise.

At Angell Memorial, we want the best for all animals. Our geriatric program is just one way to help your older cat or dog live a longer, happier life!

From the Animal Wellness Program at Angell Memorial Animal Hospital

YOUR OLDER PET

HEALTH HISTORY

Today's date:

Any medical problems that we are not aware of?

Which medications is your pet currently taking?

How is your pet's appetite?

What does your pet eat? (Include any snacks, supplements, or table food.)

Have there been any changes in your pet's eating habits or appetite recently?

Any vomiting?

Does your pet live indoors, outdoors, or both?

What kind of exercise does your pet get?

Any changes in your pet's activity level?

Does your pet cough, sneeze, or have any problem breathing associated with exercise, excitement, or nighttime?

Does your pet have problems going up or down stairs, or seem stiff at times?

Have you noticed any changes in your pet's sleeping pattern?

Does your pet pant more, and if so when?

Have you noticed any changes in your pet's behavior, vision, or hearing?

Does your pet ever have trouble chewing?

Do you ever brush your pet's teeth?

Has your pet ever had his teeth cleaned?

Any recent weight change in your pet?

Have there been any changes in water consumption or urinary habits?

Does your pet ever urinate when lying down or sleeping?

Have there been any changes in the quality, amount, or frequency of your pet's bowel movement?

Have there been any changes or problems with your pet's skin or coat? Has your pet been scratching?

Please use the diagrams to mark any unusual lumps or bumps on your pet.

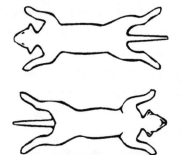

Do you have any special concerns regarding your pet?

From the Animal Wellness Program at Angell Memorial Animal Hospital

and liver function. This will allow your veterinarian to see changes more precisely.

Your dog may require a change in vaccination schedules as his body begins to slow down with age and immune function changes. This is something to discuss with your veterinarian, because it will require careful evaluation.

After the physical examination and the diagnostic tests have been completed, your veterinarian will discuss the results and explain them. Then he or she will fill out the physical examination sheet and a copy will be given to the owner. The veterinarian will also answer any questions. At Angell, the veterinarian educates the owner, teaching how to check the dog's teeth, palpate mammary glands and lymph nodes, monitor any masses that may be found, and so on. You can ask your veterinarian to teach you to do those things as well, if she hasn't asked if you'd like to learn. Your concern about your pet and interest in learning all that you can will help facilitate the client–veterinarian relationship, which will result in the optimum partnership to help keep your dog in the best possible health during his entire lifetime.

Health Maintenance for Seniors

Your senior dog will, of course, still require fresh water to be available at all times. Whether he will require a change in his diet will depend entirely on his individual condition. Not every senior dog's heart or kidneys will cause problems, so your dog may not need to eat food with adjusted salt and protein content. However, if he is less active, his diet will have to be altered accordingly in order to prevent excessive weight gain. That's a decision that your veterinarian can help you make after examining your dog and discussing his lifestyle with you. At Angell, the veterinary nutritionist calls the client within a week of the geriatric visit to discuss any nutritional concerns. This is one of the features of Angell's geriatric workup. Some helpful guidelines for feeding older dogs are shown on page 204.

YOUR OLDER PET

WELLNESS ASSESSMENT

Today's date

Temperature _____   Pulse _____   Respirations _____   Weight _____ lb

Physical Examination (N = normal, A = abnormal)

	N	A	Comments
Appearance and attitude			
Body condition			
Mucous membranes			
Eyes, ears, nose, and throat			
Lymph nodes			
Teeth, gums, mouth			
Heart/lungs			
Abdomen			
Urogenital			
Musculoskeletal			
Skin, coat, and skin tumor screen			

Vaccinations given _____

Preventive Medicine Screening Tests

Complete blood count	Blood chemistry profile
Thyroid	Heartworm
Fecal	Urinalysis
Blood pressure	Blood typing
Cytology	Chest X-rays
Other	

From the Animal Wellness Program at Angell Memorial Animal Hospital

YOUR OLDER PET

COUNSELING AND RECOMMENDATIONS

Your veterinarian will have discussed the following topics with you that relate to your pet's health. If you have any further questions or concerns, please don't hesitate to call your veterinarian, our wellness technician, our dental technician, or our nutritionist.

1. Significant abnormal lab data identified
2. Additional diagnostics recommended
   - Recheck blood tests after _____ (date)
   - Endocrine testing
   - X-rays—chest, abdomen, musculoskeletal
   - Cardiac workup
   - Additional tests
3. Dental recommendations
4. Skin and skin tumor screening
5. Musculoskeletal and exercise recommendation
6. Nutritional recommendations
   - Continue same diet
   - Change diet to _____
   - Discuss with nutritionist
7. Recheck geriatric physical exam in _____
8. Additional comments

Doctor _____

Wellness technician _____

Dental technician _____

Nutritionist _____

Please feel free to call us with questions about your pet's preventive medicine program. Thank you.

From the Animal Wellness Program at Angell Memorial Animal Hospital

This is what makes a Wellness and Preventive Medicine program special—each aspect of it is tailored to your dog's needs under his particular circumstances. There is no "one size fits all" in preventive medicine.

Your senior dog will need exercise. While some dogs are happily active well into their old age, others are best served by a slow walk around the block. Even that small amount of exercise is better than none at all. He'll enjoy the consistency of routine in his life and you'll both stay in better shape with that daily walk. He'll also enjoy sharing that time with you. When your dog is older, you and he can still share many of the things that have always been meaningful to you: perhaps a walk in a favorite place, a special treat, a boat ride on a quiet lake.

FEEDING TIPS FOR CLIENTS WITH OLDER DOGS

These general recommendations are based on the observations of many veterinarians, animal scientists, dog breeders, and owners. All dogs are individuals, however, and may be accustomed to other arrangements.

- Feed the dog in the same place at every meal. Dogs are creatures of habit, and changes in feeding routines may be especially stressful for older dogs. Choose a quiet spot where the dog will not be bothered at meal time.
- Feed at least two meals per day to older dogs. Feeding multiple, smaller meals may help overweight dogs feel more satisfied on the lower-calorie foods. In addition, it is easier for owners to monitor food intake and adjust portion size for overweight or underfed dogs when multiple meals are fed.
- Watch for any unexplained decrease in an older dog's food intake. Even if a lack of appetite does not turn out to be the first sign of a serious disease, older dogs are more vulnerable than younger dogs to the effects of inadequate nutrition from missed meals.

If you have specific questions about your pet's feeding needs, our nutritionist is available for consultation.

From the Animal Wellness Program at Angell Memorial Animal Hospital

Be sure to keep brushing your dog's teeth, and schedule an annual professional cleaning. If his teeth are dirty, a professional cleaning can revitalize him because dental problems can be discovered and corrected. Your dog can't tell you that he has a toothache, but discovering and resolving the problem will make him feel better.

Diseases of Aging

Just like aging humans, aging dogs begin to experience changes in body function. If your dog has maintained a healthy lifestyle that includes daily exercise, chances are that his heart muscle will be strong, but cardiac problems can nevertheless occur.

A diagnosis of cancer isn't unusual in a senior dog. Unfortunately, one out of every two pets over the age of ten receives that diagnosis—it is the leading cause of death in pets over the age of ten. See Chapter 12 for information that may be helpful to owners of senior dogs who must face this diagnosis and deal with the reality of the disease in their beloved companions.

Cataracts

With age comes failing vision. You may first notice an opaqueness to your dog's eyes. Or you may not be aware of changes until you realize that he's stumbling when he walks, bumping into things he would normally avoid. If your senior dog has cataracts, surgery is available and can be discussed with your veterinarian. Hearing declines with age as well. You may think your dog is ignoring you when he simply cannot hear you.

Arthritis

The word *arthritis* means inflammation of the joint(s). This disease affects dogs just as it does people, and it's every bit as uncomfortable for our canine companions. It is a degenerative joint disease (DJD) that can affect only one joint or multiple joints. It's caused by trauma, infection, abnormal chronic stresses and strains on a joint due to a variety of reasons, or the body's own antibodies forming against the joint tissue (as in rheumatoid arthritis). Older dogs are more severely affected, because the disease has had many years to progress within the joints.

Some of the signs of arthritis that your dog may exhibit are morning stiffness, exercise intolerance, limping, refusing or hesitating to climb stairs, difficulty rising from a lying-down position, or becoming more grouchy. Generally, there is no cure for chronic arthritis; however, in most cases the disease can be managed.

Your veterinarian will do some testing (blood tests, x-rays) in addition to a thorough physical examination in order to learn the cause of DJD. Treatment is generally geared to minimize the pain rather than cure the arthritis. Weight loss, a specific exercise program, a nonsteroidal, anti-inflammatory drug (NSAID), and any other joint-specific supplement recommended by your veterinarian is a common protocol for the management of arthritis. Some veterinarians will suggest acupuncture, and you may be referred to a veterinary acupuncturist.

Kidney Failure

Renal (kidney) failure is another problem often seen in aging dogs. The kidneys, like other body organs, lose function with age. The condition is diagnosed through a blood workup and a urine sample, although some dogs may be asymptomatic (not showing any signs or symptoms at all); in that case, kidney failure can only be picked up during routine geriatric screening. Symptoms include increase in thirst, weight loss, anorexia, and vomiting. Long-term treatment usually involves changing the dog's diet to one that is higher-quality, but lower in protein.

Brain Tumors

Brain tumors come from cells that are normally found in the brain or are associated with the brain. There are secondary tumors that may come from the surrounding tissues and extend into the brain, or they may come from a metastasis of primary tumors in other tissues. Growing tumors cause direct brain damage by compression and invasion of normal brain nerve cell tissue, and indirect effects of the tumor growth may cause even more significant consequences. Those secondary effects include damage to the blood-brain barrier that results in brain swelling (*edema*), and obstruction of the cerebrospinal fluid (CSF) flow. The brain is surrounded by this fluid both inside and outside; the brain floats in it and is both protected and nourished by it. The CSF is constantly being made and removed, and it flows over and through the inside of the brain, from front to back, to drain out through the spinal cord. If this flow is blocked the fluid backs up, putting pressure on the brain and damaging it. It can cause hemorrhage and secondary hydrocephalus, brain herniation caused by pressure from the enlarging mass.

Brain tumors usually manifest neurologic signs that vary with the location of the tumor. For example, tumors occurring in the forebrain will usually cause seizures. The dog will likely exhibit such signs as circling, behavioral abnormalities, poor vision, and poor posture.

Depending on the location and type of brain tumor, many dogs can be treated with surgical removal of the tumor, radiation therapy, or chemotherapy.

Canine Cognitive Dysfunction

Canine cognitive dysfunction (CCD) is commonly thought to be the canine version of Alzheimer's disease. In dogs it can be confused with separation anxiety and, indeed, separation anxiety may play a part in CCD or be a precursor to it. There is no absolute answer to why this happens, or why it happens to some dogs and not others. The brains of both humans and dogs with cognitive dysfunction have been reported to contain beta-amyloid plaques, and researchers think these plaques lead to nerve cell damage and dementia.

A dog with CCD will have any combination of a variety of symptoms. He may forget where he is, getting lost in his own home. He may begin to bark for no reason, he may sleep more, and he may no longer want to be petted. He may not be as interested in eating as he once was. Heartbreakingly, as with Alzheimer's patients, he may no longer recognize family members. The dog may also forget his housetraining (although this can certainly be symptomatic of another illness, such as urinary tract infection or urinary incontinence), and he may no longer be able to find his way to the door.

Medication is available to treat canine cognitive dysfunction—discuss this with your veterinarian. Some dogs respond well to it, and it restores them to their former happy state; others respond less favorably but do show some improvement; still others do not respond at all. The medication does take some time to take effect. There are new veterinary diets that are formulated to aid cognitive function.

Diet and the Senior Dog

Diet plays a big part in your dog's health, and senior dogs have unique nutritional needs due to different disease processes that can occur in them. If your senior dog is perfectly healthy, he may not need any change in diet. Dogs who maintain a healthy lifestyle throughout their lives may continue into their senior years with very few, if any, problems. However, if your dog experiences age-related problems like cardiac or kidney disease, your veterinarian may recommend a veterinary diet.

In recent years we've seen a trend of antioxidants being added to pet foods for the purpose of controlling free radicals. Free radicals are damaged molecules that kill invading viruses but can also destroy healthy cells. Free radicals are usually produced by normal metabolism or absorbed from the environment, and they will damage cells during the aging process. This is not just true of dogs but of all species, including humans. It's now known that antioxidants help counterbalance damage done to cells by free radicals. By adding antioxidants such as Vitamins C and E and many others to the diet, the antioxidants "absorb" and counteract free radicals before they can do damage. Recent research has shown that senior dogs, when fed a diet containing anitoxidants, exhibited a greater ability to perform specific tasks than their counterparts in a control group who were fed a regular balanced diet without antioxidants.

Making Life Simpler

The changes your dog experiences as he ages may make him more anxious. If your dog experienced separation anxiety when he was young, he will very likely experience it as a senior. Even if he didn't have separation anxiety as a puppy or young dog, he is very likely to exhibit the symptoms now.

The loss of hearing and eyesight can make him justifiably nervous. You may be close by, but he may perceive that closeness as being entirely too far away. He may become clingy and overly attached to you. He is now more dependent than ever before and understands that his world has changed. Things that were once clear are no longer so, and that can be worrisome to your dog.

There are things you can do to make his world a more comfortable place. These things require a little effort and thoughtfulness, but they will go a long way toward helping your dog enjoy his senior years. If your dog is experiencing a loss of vision, you might put a strip of carpeting or fabric at the doorway to the room where he enjoys spending time. If he can feel the difference in the texture, it will make getting around much easier. Be sure to tack it down so he and other family members won't trip and injure themselves. Also, this is not the time to rearrange the furniture. It's best to leave the furniture as it is because he's familiar with it, and it will be easier for him to navigate the house without bumping into chairs and couches that have been moved to unfamiliar locations.

Lack of complete vision will probably make him more anxious at night when everyone is asleep. He may have to get up and walk to another room for a drink of water, and nightlights can help to light his way and make him more sure of himself and his surroundings. Leaving a nightlight on in the room where he sleeps will also make him feel more comfortable.

Failing vision may mean that your dog won't see you when you enter the room. Try to remember to let him know that you're there by speaking to him if he's not looking in your direction, or if he can't see at all. If his hearing is also failing, you'll have to alert him in some other fashion. Some dogs can still hear if you clap your hands loudly, while others with complete hearing loss will appreciate it if you stamp on the floor when you enter the room. The dog who cannot hear can still feel the vibrations and will know that you're in the room. It's far kinder than startling him by touching him without letting him know that you're coming close to him.

On the other hand, he may develop noise phobia. It's sometimes possible to prevent or control the noise; sometimes it's not, but you may be able to find an area of the house where the noise is less bothersome, or you may be able to enact a desensitization program with the help of your veterinarian. Noise phobia should begin to abate when your dog begins the normal process of hearing loss.

Tricks of the Trade

Adding an extra water dish or two is helpful for the senior dog. Your canine friend may not feel like walking all the way to another part of the house to get a drink. Having an extra water dish in another room can help to make his life a little easier.

If your dog can no longer climb up on the bed or the sofa, he doesn't have to forgo those places, especially since they will be more comfortable for him than a hard floor. You can buy, or make, steps or a ramp that can be put at the side of the bed or sofa to assist him in attaining his goal. Alternately, you can pile up pillows to help him in his ascent. This trick will also be helpful in getting your larger dog into the car or van. It's easy to pick up a small dog and put him into the car, but a big dog will need some help. And don't forget to have some soft bedding in the car for him to make his travels more comfortable.

Keep your older pet warm and comfortable. He will probably feel the cold more at this stage of his life, just as older people do, so blankets and sweaters will be appreciated. Be sure that his bedding is comfortable. Egg crate–style mattress covers are available in dog beds to take pressure off an achy, arthritic body. There are also heated dog beds, or heat packs that may be used as part of daily therapy. You may also want to see if massage and therapeutic swimming are available for dogs in your area. It's important to get his muscles and joints moving again, and those are very good ways of doing it.

Elderly dogs, like elderly people, may not respond well to change in their environment or routine. The addition of a new family member, whether it's an infant or a spouse, may be bothersome to an elderly dog, as might a change in the owner's daily schedule. If you have always gotten up early and now sleep later, for example, your dog may not be able to adjust well to the change. If the family has to move, it may very well be that the dog won't adjust quickly or well to the new home. These changes that are simple for the owner may cause behavior problems in the senior dog as a result of either physical problems or degenerative changes.

Your older dog may react slowly now. Many older dogs still enjoy playing and want that special interaction with their owner. The dog who can't play fetch will enjoy catching a rolled ball and bringing it back for praise and love. If your dog has lost his sight, you can use a ball with a bell in it so he'll have an auditory cue. You can kick such a ball on the grass to allow some low-level running and cardiac stimulation without jarring activity. He might enjoy playing with a stuffed toy, or a biscuit ball. That sort of stimulation will help make his days more enjoyable and interesting.

Your dog may fail to react as he once did. For example, he may well be confused when you throw a toy, wondering exactly what just sailed past him. This doesn't mean that he no longer has quality of life, it just means that he is no longer a candidate for a game of fetch. He might prefer to simply lie near you and enjoy your company.

If, on the other hand, your dog is experiencing pain due to an organic problem, such as arthritis, he may become anxious or irritable when touched. Or he may exhibit signs of aggressiveness or fear as a result of pain. Aggression is usually fear-based, so it's not hard to imagine that the fear of being unable to see or hear well, combined with pain, could cause the dog to react more aggressively.

Report any behavioral changes to your veterinarian as soon as they appear so she can do a medical workup to evaluate the situation and see whether an organic problem is the cause. As with puppies and middle-aged dogs, the sooner a diagnosis is made, the sooner treatment can begin.

What We've Learned

Cognitive: Referring to mental function
Edema: An abnormal accumulation of fluid that causes swelling
Palpate: To feel with the hand
Phobia: A persistent, abnormal dread or fear

14

Saying Goodbye

**When you are very close, it is difficult to
separate out emotions when the end is near.
It is understandable and normal to want to
keep your pet forever. When a decision is needed,
try to always use your pet's quality of life as your guide.**
—Peter Theran, V.M.D.,
Diplomate, A.C.V.I.M.

There's a lifetime of bonding, a relationship that grows stronger by the day as you and your dog learn more about each other. Your dog is now the companion you've always wanted, and life is sweet. But you also know that the years are growing shorter. Each day is a special gift with your beloved dog.

Life Expectancy

Death can come at any time. No matter how well one plans, no matter how carefully one cares for a beloved companion animal, accidents can occur, as can catastrophic illnesses. It's important to understand that it is possible that your pet will die at a relatively young age. Some veterinarians, in fact, will remind owners early on that a pet's life is finite. No matter how fervently we wish that our companion animals would live forever, the truth is that they don't, that their lifespan is far shorter than our own.

A dog's lifespan is affected by her size—small dogs live much longer than large-breed dogs, and Giant breeds typically have very short lifespans. While a small dog may live to be seventeen years or older, a Giant breed may not live beyond seven or eight years. Other factors in a dog's life expectancy include her general health and the all-important issue of quality of life.

Preparing for Loss

Loss is something pet owners should prepare themselves for. Owners need to become acquainted with the scope of their responsibilities as caregivers and reconcile the ethical and moral dilemmas that inevitably come at a time when emotions are running high. Waiting until there is a crisis before making life-or-death decisions is not the best way to sort out the issues.

When the owner has always done whatever it takes to keep the animal well, it's difficult to accept that there comes a time when no more can be done. As difficult as it may be to face the truth—and it is so much easier to slip into denial—it's far easier to begin to prepare for the loss and to begin to accept that it is inevitable than to be caught up in a whirlwind of pain while trying to make decisions. The decisions and the pain will be difficult enough without postponing them and refusing to face the reality of the situation: that life has an ending as well as a beginning.

Learning to recognize quality of life, and when that no longer exists, can go a long way in easing the mental distress and second-guessing that so often consume people after euthanizing their pets. They anguish over their decision, tormenting themselves and wondering whether they euthanized the dog too soon or too late. They feel guilty that they have "killed" their dog, or that they might have prolonged the dog's suffering. It's best to accept beforehand this important distinction: euthanasia is a determination of *how* an animal will die, rather than *whether* the animal will die.

Euthanasia

It's sad when an elderly dog dies of natural causes, and it is normal to mourn that loss. But the issue becomes more complex when the owner must choose to euthanize a beloved pet. We all prefer that our companion animals die of natural causes; we hope that they will slip quietly away in sleep one night. But that rarely happens. When a dog's quality of life deteriorates to a certain point, the owner is put in the position of making a life-or-death decision, and that's a heavy burden. There are times when the last gift you can give a beloved companion animal is the gift of release from pain and anguish and a poor quality of life.

Knowing when the time is right is the key to making this significant decision. Some pet owners instinctively know when it's time for euthanasia. The common expression is, "The dog will tell you when it's time." And, indeed, the human–animal bond is such that the owner can often tell when quality of life no longer exists, and they seem to be able to "read" the dog and understand that the dog wants release from pain and suffering, that the dog has an understanding that it's time.

But you don't have to rely on instinct alone. Consult your veterinarian with regard to pursuing and understanding your dog's medical condition; ask if it's associated with pain. It's also important to understand clinical signs such as shortness of breath, disorientation, and seizures, and how they might influence the decision to euthanize your dog. There is medication available for pain, and once pain is alleviated the dog can continue to have quality of life.

Often veterinarians feel very uncomfortable in broaching the subject of this responsibility for euthanasia, as do owners. But it's important to realize that domestic animals, because they live with us, are deprived of the forces of nature that would otherwise prove fatal to them. Of course, we wouldn't have it any other way, but it does place the responsibility for recognizing quality of life squarely on our shoulders. It's not uncommon for the pet owner to ask the veterinarian what he would do if this were his dog. The owner is looking for reassurance that she's doing the right thing at the right time.

Knowing what sort of preparations must be made will at the very least allow the pet owner to make some basic decisions before the inevitable. Not only will the owner learn to recognize when quality of life no longer exists, but there will be an opportunity to think clearly about such choices as burial—for example, Where will the burial be? Is it allowed by law to be in the owner's yard, or must it be in a pet cemetery? What about cremation? It's important to decide how you want to memorialize your dog to express your enduring love for your companion and that special relationship you shared.

You might want to ask about how the euthanasia procedure takes place, and think about whether you want a necropsy (autopsy) performed on your pet. And you'll have to decide whether you want to be present when your pet is euthanized. Holding your dog at this time, or allowing her head to rest in your lap while you stroke her, is very comforting for both the dog and the owner, but some people cannot handle it. There's nothing wrong with admitting that you cannot do it. You have to do whatever makes you comfortable, whatever you can live with after the fact.

Whether or not you choose to be present when your dog is euthanized, most veterinarians will allow you time alone with your pet beforehand in order to say goodbye. That quiet time allows you to come to terms with

VISITING YOUR DOG

If the dog is hospitalized, it's important to visit, not just for the dog's sake but for the owner's sake as well. Just like any other patient, a dog wants to know that loved ones are near. And if the illness is fatal, or potentially fatal, visiting will help to prepare the owner for the possibility of death as an outcome.

the inevitable outcome and to talk to your beloved dog one last time, per-haps expressing feelings about your relationship and what it has meant and how much love you've shared. What each owner chooses to say is very personal. Some will say nothing at all, but just being able to hold the dog and hug her one last time is meaningful.

It's important to explore the significance of your relationship with your dog. Even people who have children will often view their dog as a child. Your bond with your dog will last long after the dog is no longer alive; the memories will always be special.

Dealing with Grief

Since an individual's grief is an ongoing process, it is important to culti-vate support within oneself. Too many people make excuses for themselves and don't respect their own grief. It's important that you care for yourself in your grief. You are losing a friend, a family member. The relationship you have with your dog is unique and significant, and deserves respect.

There's no shame in grieving for a pet who is, after all, a much-loved family member. In fact, many people have found that they will cry for the loss of a pet when they have been unable to cry over the loss of a relative; the pet's loss may become a catalyst for that grieving process as well.

It's important to have a social support network, at least one friend or relative to whom you can turn and openly express your feelings without fear of ridicule or being told "It's just a dog." Your companion is not "just a dog." Angell offers two support groups, called Approaching Loss and Coping with Loss, that provide a safe haven for your grief to be expressed.

Accept how you feel, appreciate the relationship for what it has been and the joy that it has brought, and know that your life has been enriched because of your pet.

Whether and when you will choose to bring another dog into your life is a purely personal matter. For some people, there will never be another dog. Others may choose to bring home another dog immediately, or within months. For some people, it takes years to decide that the time is

SEVEN TIPS FOR DEALING WITH GRIEF

1. Accept your sadness. It is natural and normal to experience intense grief over the loss of a pet that is valued as a vital part of one's family.

2. Don't expect to grieve according to some preset plan. The depth and duration of one's grief are unique to the individual and the specific relationship that has been shared with a particular animal.

3. Grief imposes many challenges to one's physical as well as emotional and spiritual well-being. Be mindful of the self-care that is essential to healing, being attentive to one's needs for proper nutrition, adequate rest, and relaxing activity.

4. While it can be a relief to express your thoughts and feelings about the pet's lifetime to empathic others for support, it is critically important to be respectful and supportive of oneself, acknowledging the devoted care that you have provided throughout the pet's life.

5. Honor the emotions you experience for your pet. Bolster your understanding of this specific and very special relationship through readings and discussions that enhance understanding and appreciation of human–animal bonding in general.

6. As you begin to adjust to the physical absence of the dearly loved pet, you will find the bond you forged to be continuously enriching. Create a journal of notes about the values and teachings that your beloved pet has inspired for you.

7. Your pet may have cultivated a strong awareness of the fulfillment that can be derived from mutual love and caring. It is this fundamental need that will guide you toward renewing energies to develop sources for further joys to be discovered again.

right to open their home and heart to another canine companion, to accept the responsibility for another life with all that it brings. And all that it brings is, in the end, wonderful. It's a shared journey, a relationship like no other.

What We've Learned

Euthanasia: The act of painlessly putting to death a hopelessly sick or injured animal, as an act of mercy

Necropsy: An autopsy on an animal

Resources

Following are some reliable sources to give you further information on topics covered in this book.

Websites

AKC Canine Health Foundation (the only health foundation devoted
    solely to research projects for the health of dogs)
    akcchf.org
The American Animal Hospital Association
    healthypet.com
The American Veterinary Medical Association
    avma.org
Merck Veterinary Manual (online edition)
    merckvetmanual.com
PetDiets.com
    petdiets.com
The Pet Place
    petplace.com

Books

Grief

Coping with Sorrow on the Loss of Your Pet, Moira Anderson. Alpine
  Publications, 1996.
Goodbye Friend, Gary Kowalski. Stillpoint Publishing, 1997.
Pet Loss: A Thoughtful Guide for Adults and Children, Herbert Nieberg
  and Arlene Fisher. Montgomery Press, 1982.
*Preparing for the Loss of Your Pet: Saying Goodbye with Love, Dignity, and
  Peace of Mind*, Myrna Milani, D.V.M. Prima Publishing, 1998.

Training and Behavior

The Bark Stops Here, Terry Ryan. Legacy-by-Mail, Inc., 2000.
Clicker Training for Dogs, Karen Pryor. Sunshine Books, 2001.
Clicker Training for Obedience, Morgan Spector. Sunshine Books, 1999.
Don't Shoot the Dog, Karen Pryor. Bantam Books, 1999.
On Talking Terms with Dogs: Calming Signals, Turid Rugaas. Hanalei,
  1997.
Quick Clicks, Mandy Book and Cheryl S. Smith. Hanalei, 2001.

Veterinary Medical Reference

Merck Veterinary Manual (8th edition), Merck & Company, 1998.

Videos

Clicker Magic!, Sunshine Books, 1996.
Take a Bow Wow: Easy Tricks Any Dog Can Do!, Take a Bow Wow, 1995.

About the Contributors

Executive Editor: Paul C. Gambardella, V.M.D., M.S., Diplomate, A.C.V.S.

After graduating from the University of Pennsylvania, Paul C. Gambardella, V.M.D., M.S., Diplomate, A.C.V.S., did his internship and surgical residency at the University of Minnesota from 1973 to 1975. He was associate professor of surgery and head of small animal surgery at Tufts University School of Veterinary Medicine from 1981 to 1985, and clinical professor of surgery from 1985 until 2001. He was a staff surgeon at Angell Memorial Animal Hospital from 1975 to 1980, director of surgery from 1984 to 1989, and Angell's chief of staff from 1989 to 2001.

Dr. Gambardella has authored twenty-two scientific articles and several book chapters, and he lectures widely. He is a past president of the American College of Veterinary Surgeons (1994–1995) and the New England Veterinary Medical Association (1995–1996). Dr. Gambardella received the American Animal Hospital Association (AAHA) Award for Outstanding Service, Region 1, in 1986, and AAHA's FIDO Award as Veterinarian of the Year in 1998. He assumed the post of hospital director at Oradell Animal Hospital in New Jersey on February 1, 2002.

Senior Editor: Douglas Brum, D.V.M.

Following his 1985 graduation from Cornell University School of Veterinary Medicine, Douglas Brum, D.V.M., did his internship at Angell Memorial Animal Hospital from 1985 to 1986, then spent one year in private practice in the Boston area. He returned to Angell in 1987, where he is now a senior staff member. He was director of the internship program from 1988 to 1993. Dr. Brum started the Wellness Clinic in 1993 and has served as its director since then. In 1993 he received the Mary Mitchell Humane Award.

Contributing Editors

Maria Glowaski, D.V.M., Diplomate, A.C.V.A., served as head of anesthesiology at Angell Memorial Animal Hospital. She is currently Adjunct Clinical Associate Professor in Anesthesiology at Tufts University School of Veterinary Medicine, where she received her D.V.M. The author of a forthcoming book on veterinary anesthesia, Dr. Glowaski has authored several anesthesia publications as well as chapters in anesthesia textbooks. She has also lectured at national veterinary meetings.

Kathleen Kalaher, D.V.M., Diplomate, A.C.V.D., is a 1982 graduate of the New York State College of Veterinary Medicine at Cornell University. She completed an internship at Angell Memorial Animal Hospital from 1982 to 1983, and, after four years in private practice, returned to Cornell from 1987 to 1989 to complete a residency in veterinary dermatology. She has been a board-certified diplomate in the American College of Veterinary Dermatology since 1991, and has over twelve years of experience in both university and private referral practice settings.

Jane N. Nathanson, L.C.S.W., L.R.C., C.R.C., is licensed and certified in social work and rehabilitation. She has twenty-five years' experience providing counseling and consulting services. Her areas of specialization include crisis and stress management and loss, grief, and adjustment counseling. Nathanson has fifteen years' experience providing counseling and consulting services with regard to human–animal bonding and related animal caregiving issues for individuals, humane services organizations, veterinary schools, and hospitals. She established the Pet Loss Support Program for the MSPCA in 1990 and has since conducted its group and individual services.

Karen Overall, M.A., V.M.D., Ph.D., received her B.A. and M.A. degrees concomitantly from the University of Pennsylvania in 1978. She was awarded her V.M.D. from the University of Pennsylvania School of Veterinary Medicine in 1983 and completed a residency in behavioral medicine at Penn in 1989, and her Ph.D. in zoology from the University of Wisconsin—Madison in 1997. Dr. Overall has given hundreds of national and international presentations and short courses, and is the author of over 100 scholarly publications. She has been a regular columnist for both *Canine Practice* and *Feline Practice* and currently writes a bimonthly column for *DVM Newsmagazine*. She has authored two textbooks: *Clinical Behavioral Medicine for Small Animals* (Mosby, 1997) and *Manual of Small Animal Behavioral Medicine* (Elsevier, 2003). She is a diplomate of the American College of Veterinary Behavior (ACVB) and is certified by the Animal Behavior Society (ABS) as an applied animal behaviorist. She spent fourteen years at the University of Pennsylvania School of Veterinary Medicine, where she ran the behavior clinic for twelve years. Dr. Overall frequently consults with service dog organizations, including narcotic dog groups, Guide Dogs for the Blind, and Canine Companions for Independence. She also has consulted with lawmakers regarding legislation affecting dogs. She was awarded the 1993 Randy Award for Excellence and Creativity in Research. Dr. Overall is currently a research associate in the Psychiatry Department at the University of Pennsylvania School of Medicine.

Rebecca L. Remillard, Ph.D., D.V.M., Diplomate, A.C.V.N., earned her Ph.D. from Colorado State University in 1983. She graduated from Tufts

University School of Veterinary Medicine in 1987 and went on to become board certified in veterinary nutrition in 1991. She was appointed clinical nutritionist at Angell Memorial Animal Hospital in 1993. Dr. Remillard has lectured nationally and has published extensively.

William Rosenblad, D.V.M., graduated from Tufts University School of Veterinary Medicine in 1995. He did an internship in general medicine and surgery at The Animal Medical Center in New York City and then completed a residency in veterinary dentistry at the University of Pennsylvania School of Veterinary Medicine. Dr. Rosenblad has been on the staff of the surgery/dentistry department at Angell Memorial since 1998. He has lectured and been a lab instructor at various venues.

Allen Sisson, D.V.M., M.S., Diplomate, A.C.V.I.M. (neurology), graduated from Ohio State University. He did an internship at Angell Memorial Animal Hospital from 1978 to 1979. He practiced at a small animal hospital in New Jersey from 1979 to 1980 and then returned to Angell Memorial, where he was a staff member with a specialty in neurology and internal medicine from 1980 to 1987. He completed a residency in neurology and neurosurgery at the College of Veterinary Medicine, Colorado State University, from 1987 to 1990. He returned to Angell and from 1990 to 1993 was a staff member specializing in neurology and neurosurgery. After a brief stint at the Veterinary Hospital of San Diego in 1993, he returned to Angell, where he is once again a staff member specializing in neurology and neurosurgery.

Index